AUDEMARS, PIGUET
GENÈVE

SWISS

THE **WATCH**

GENE STONE

ABRAMS, NEW YORK

Project Manager: Eric Himmel
Editor: Tricia Levi
Designer: Miko McGinty
Production Manager: Anet Sirna-Bruder

LIBRARY OF CONGRESS CATALOGING-IN-PUBLICATION DATA

Stone, Gene.
  The watch / by Gene Stone.
    p. cm.

  ISBN 13: 978-0-8109-3093-3 (hardcover)
  ISBN 10: 0-8109-3093-5

1. Wrist watches. 2. Wrist watches — Collectors and collecting. I. Title.

  NK7489.S76 2006
  681.1'14—dc22

                    2006016970

Printed and bound in China

10 9 8 7 6 5 4 3 2 1

HNA ▌▌▌▌▌
harry n. abrams, inc.
a subsidiary of La Martinière Groupe
115 West 18th Street
New York, NY 10011
www.hnabooks.com

FRONT ENDSHEET: World War II military watches from the collection of Steve Gurevitz

PAGE 1: Audemars Piguet Ultrathin, 1940s, yellow gold, mechanical movement

PAGE 2: Blancpain Chronometer, 1980s, detail of dial

PAGE 3: Philippe Dufour Simplicity, 2000s, detail of movement

PAGE 4: Franck Muller Endurance 24, 1999, white gold, mechanical movement with chronograph (left); Hublot Big Bang, 2005, stainless steel, titanium, and ceramic, self-winding mechanical movement with chronograph and date (right)

PAGE 5: Maurice Lacroix Régulateur, 2000s, stainless steel and pink gold, self-winding mechanical movement with date and second time zone (left); Ulysse Nardin 1846 Marine Diver Chronometer, c. 2005, stainless steel, self-winding mechanical movement with date and power-reserve indicator (right)

THIS PAGE: Two rare pieces — a gold Rolex Cellini coin watch (1980) and a stainless-steel Rolex golfer's watch (early 1930s)

OPPOSITE: Patek Philippe Ref. 1491, 1940s, yellow gold, mechanical movement

PAGE 22: Vacheron Constantin, 1950s, pink gold, mechanical movement with chronograph

PAGE 23: Bell & Ross Vintage 126, 2000s, detail of movement

PAGE 224: Patek Philippe Ref. 5000, 1990s, detail of movement

PAGE 225: Baume & Mercier Riviera, 2000s, stainless steel, self-winding mechanical movement with chronograph and date

PAGE 242: Omega Seamaster cal. 321 chronograph movement

BACK ENDSHEET: Dress watches from the collection of Mort Janklow

Contents

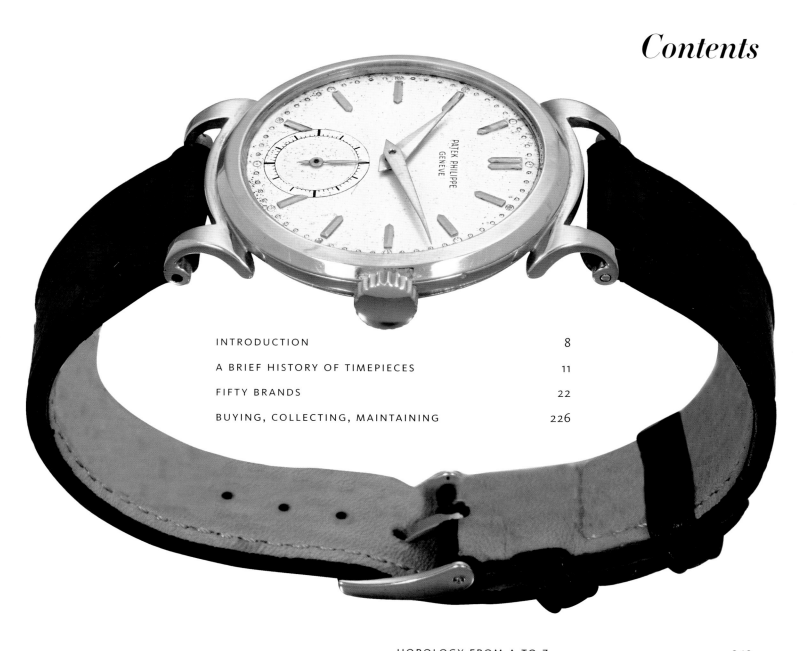

INTRODUCTION

What is a man's wristwatch? Is it a piece of jewelry? A mechanical marvel? A fashion accessory? Or a fashion necessity?

It all depends on its owner. For many men, a wristwatch is the only piece of jewelry they'll ever own. It's a chance for those who disdain a chain or an earring to wear a precious metal — gold, silver, or platinum. Men who feel uncomfortable even with a bland school ring will wear a huge solid-gold Audemars Piguet or Vacheron Constantin.

Then again, many men will tell you that a watch isn't a piece of jewelry at all. It is a practical device worn for a sole reason: to tell the time. Jewelry is a trifle, whereas a watch is a necessity. Many of these men are fond of quartz watches because of their accuracy, and opt for Japanese brands such as Citizen and Seiko, or the German Junghans, which manufactures radio-controlled timepieces.

For others, the wristwatch is a complicated piece of machinery. And the more complicated, the better. These are men who want the newest innovations in chronographs, calendars, power reserves, repeaters, and tourbillons. IWC's Il Destriero Scafusia is a split-seconds chronograph with a tourbillon that tells hours, minutes, seconds, day, date, moon phases, year, and also contains an hour, quarter-hour, and minute repeater. This model sold out. And watches with even more complications have been introduced.

Given that the watch is often the only item a discreet man can wear that shows off his wealth, some consider a watch the equivalent of a fancy sports car for the wrist. In these circles, a watch offers men the chance to roll up their sleeves and prove their worth with a huge piece of glitter, such as a Franck Muller or a Roger Dubuis.

And then there are those for whom wearing a watch is a chance to prove that they possess the latest, hippest invention: a device that not only tells time, but also features accessories like a temperature measurement function, a heart-rate monitor, and tidal information, such as the Casio G-Shock model line, whose instruction manuals are thicker than many books.

A watch is also a piece of history. To own a watch is to own the latest evolution of a record of timekeeping dating back to water clocks and sundials — it's a tiny replica of the same mechanism used by medieval clocks six hundred years ago. Some of the watches from companies like Jaquet Droz or A. Lange & Söhne purposefully look like timepieces of yore — and these, too, often sell out.

A watch can represent a slice of family history, too. A friend of mine has a gold Patek Philippe that his grandfather bought in 1925. Then his father wore it (only on special occasions — he considered his Longines more useful for day-to-day wear). Now my friend owns the Patek Philippe — but as the company's own advertising slogan boasts, you don't own a Patek Philippe as much as you pass it along to the next generation.

But of course, if you don't want to pass the watch along, you can sell it. That's yet another category of watch: the appreciable investment. Unlike a refrigerator, which loses value the moment it's purchased, a well-bought watch can gain value. A 14-karat-gold Hamilton Otis that cost $67.50 in 1938 can fetch $10,000 today.

For the less financially minded, a watch is a fashion accessory to be matched with a belt and shoes. Such men disparage the notion that one can wear a brown leather band with black shoes and belt, or vice versa. A watch, whatever its brand or price, is a detail in an outfit, and at times a $50 vintage watch can be more correct than a $10,000 Rolex if the rest of the attire complements it.

Finally, a watch is an aesthetic pleasure. What do you look at more often each day than your watch? Why not wear on your wrist something that makes you happy whenever you see it? Aesthetes aren't interested in its movement, or how it corresponds to their clothes, or even whether it keeps good time. For them, the face is everything.

For all watch wearers, the timepiece is still something else. Everyone finds himself alone at some point, in an unfamiliar environment or in a strange place: the terrible hotel room you're given when a flight is cancelled, the motel room that's never been cleaned. These are the times when you know that, even if your clothes are rumpled, the phones aren't working, and the lighting is ominous, you have a companion. You take out your small piece of metallic genius and gaze at it. You feel a sense of pride in its workmanship, a sense of familiarity with its face, a sense of attachment to its touch.

A wristwatch is a universe of possibilities. It is a metaphor for the cosmos or a nice hunk of gold. It is anything and everything you want it to be. Wear it, stare at it, love it, repair it, open it, time it: Your watch represents a small part of you, wherever you go.

Gene Stone

RIGHT: **A PIECE OF JEWELRY . . .**
Vacheron Constantin 222, 1980s, yellow gold and stainless steel, self-winding mechanical movement with date

FAR RIGHT: **THE MORE COMPLICATED, THE BETTER . . .** IWC Il Destriero Scafusia, 2000s, pink gold, mechanical self-winding movement with tourbillon, split-seconds chronograph, perpetual calendar, minute repeater, and moon-phase indicator

FAR LEFT: **A PRACTICAL DEVICE . . .** Citizen Calibre 2100, 2000s, titanium, Eco-Drive movement with chronograph, date, alarm, and power-reserve indicator

LEFT: **A SLICE OF HISTORY . . .** Patek Philippe, 1926, yellow gold, mechanical movement

BREGUET, PARIS, c. 1790, silver, mechanical movement with date

A BRIEF HISTORY OF TIMEPIECES

The urge to know time predates recorded history. Primitive people left no accounts, but we know that as humankind began to develop complicated social structures, the coordination of time became increasingly important. Social cooperation demands structure: People wishing to hunt, fish, or farm together need to be able to coordinate when to start and stop, as they do for any other mutual events planned for a future time.

For eons, the sky and the clock were virtually synonymous. The sun, the moon, and the stars calculated time for those observant enough to understand. Knowing cosmology meant the ability to determine when the weather was going to become cold or warm, when the seasons would change, and any other events vital to civilization.

Humans responded by becoming avid timekeepers; some of the largest and most impressive of early man-made structures — the Egyptian pyramids (which predict equinoxes) and Stonehenge (which foretells any number of seasonal aspects) — were designed in part to keep track of time. They had other functions as well — some obvious (the pyramids were tombs), others not so obvious (Stonehenge's ultimate purpose is still unknown). These monuments were also among the earliest public clocks.

For most of human history, the division of time took place on this large scale — seasonally, monthly, weekly. But as civilization grew more complicated, the need to divide the day into smaller increments arose. The Egyptians were the first to come up with the twenty-four-hour day, and later the Greeks and Romans followed suit. These hours, based on the solar day, were not equal — the twelve daylight hours were longer than the twelve nighttime hours in the summer, and the opposite in the winter.

Similarly, the first so-called clocks — mostly time sticks and sundials — were not accurate to the degree modern civilization expects and requires. Sundials have spokes (also called gnomon) that cast a slim shadow; time was told by judging its angle and length. Originally simple, these sun-dials grew ornate, with hour markers carved into the earth or upon a highly decorated metal base. Form became as important as function; a simple dial could tell the time as well as a fancier one, but increasingly the preference favored elaborate models, just as today watches that merely report the time are less popular than watches with fancy embellishments. Some fashions don't change.

Because sundials only work if the sky is clear and the sun bright, early timekeepers searched out other ways to indicate the passage of time. These included marking a candle with bands that burned at specified rates, and the development of the hourglass, filled with sand seeping through a small hole in a predictable trickle.

Other inventions followed, perhaps the most successful being the water clock, or *clepsydra*, a 3000 BC Chinese invention that tracks the flow of water into a vertical tank at marked intervals, like sand through an hourglass. Western societies eventually adopted it. The Egyptians used the clepsydra as early as 1500 BC, and Plato introduced it to the Greeks.

The mechanics behind these water clocks were simple, but like sundials, clepsydras evolved into ornate structures (the Egyptians jeweled their nozzles). Many were supplied with the latest innovations in gears and dials, and some sprouted extra functions such as hour-tolling or displaying planets' orbits.

———

Between the fall of ancient civilizations and the rise of Western society, the face of timekeeping history becomes almost blank once again. In Europe, few people needed to know the time, nor had the ingenuity or the means to

NOURRISSON À LYON, 1659, silver and gold, sundial with compass. Sundials, often combined with compasses, preceded watches as portable timekeepers, but they can't have been very practical.

build complicated machines of any kind. Timekeeping methods did not change dramatically for many centuries, although the Chinese continued to work on their water-driven clocks. Inventor Su Song (c. AD 1088) created water clocks with complex astronomical displays and chimes; his drawings were so detailed that recently scientists were able to build one of his devices.

But, as records from the twelfth and thirteenth centuries indicate, interest in the timepiece, or horologium, began to resurface. And in the fourteenth century, mechanical clocks made their first appearance in Europe.

————

The invention that made it possible to build a mechanical clock is a device called an escapement. The escapement translates the anarchic, onrushing energy generated by a primitive power source like a falling weight or, later, a powerful spring, into the gentle, metronomic pulses needed to keep a clock running accurately.

The French architect Villard de Honnecourt described an escapement as early as AD 1250, but there's no record to prove he actually built a clock containing one. The first clocks with an escapement seem to have appeared in Europe in the late thirteenth century. No one knows exactly who first invented them, or where; England, Flanders, Italy, and France lead the list of possibilities. Norwich, England, had a clock tower by 1352; St. Albans, near London, had one by mid-century; and in Italy, a famous astronomical clock, constructed by Giovanni de Dondi, was completed in 1364.

Then again, as historian David S. Landes points out in his book *Revolution in Time*, it's also possible that Pope Sylvester II (c. 940–1003) built a mechanical clock. No one knows.

These early clocks were indebted to their water-clock predecessors in that they used the same weight-driven gears previously employed to ring bells on water clocks or other non-mechanical devices; added to that were the gears of an early escapement.

These clocks had no hands, however. Their purpose was to ring bells to sound the hours, which is probably why the word clock derives from the Old French word *clocke*, which in turn comes from the Medieval Latin *clocca*; both words mean bell.

Slowly, hands and wheels came into alignment, and by later in the fourteenth century large clocks with hour hands were being built throughout Europe.

Which came first, the ability to create a device that could tell the time to any human who wanted to know, or the human desire to own a device that could do so? Was history altered by the sudden ability to know time, or did society need timepieces in order to help structure the changes already taking place?

The questions are unanswerable. But the ability to know the time in a more personal way than had ever been possible before was a development with major ramifications for the workplace, communications, transportation, and the military, all of which were better able to operate with uniform timekeeping.

By the sixteenth century, a great many clocks had been built, but these were large and public. The first mechanism that could be considered a watch didn't appear until 1511 when, according to some horologists, a German named Peter Henlein created a pocket watch with a single hour hand; it was called the Nuremberg Egg. Others claim that the Italians had already invented a portable clock in the late fifteenth century. But because timekeeping and record-keeping were on the same track — making advances, but still relatively primitive — we may never know for sure.

The primary problem inventors faced while creating a portable timepiece was the driving power. Most timepieces of the day were driven by weights, which were not portable. But rapidly developing advancements in metallurgy allowed the manufacture of small, oiled springs, which were eventually able to take the place of the traditional weights. (At the time, both stationary and portable timekeepers used what's known as a foliot, which would eventually be replaced by the pendulum in stationary clocks, to maintain an even rate. The foliot eventually evolved into the balance wheel, combined with a coiled hairspring, in portable timekeepers.)

Small clocks slowly grew in popularity, especially among royalty. Emperor Charles V commissioned several, and in France, watchmaker Julien Coudrey supposedly made two daggers with small clocks enclosed in their handles for King Louis XI.

Most of these early efforts were German or French — the Swiss and the English did not begin making pocket watches until later in the century; one of the earliest English

UNKNOWN MAKER, THE NATIVITY, c. 1600, gilt bronze and silver, mechanical movement. This clock, made to hang as a pendant, predates the invention of the balance spring.

pieces may well have been the watch set in a bracelet that the Earl of Leicester presented to Queen Elizabeth in 1571.

Portable watches were most often worn as pendants around the neck, although some were small enough to be cased in precious metals and worn as a ring. And, like Elizabeth's watch, some were strapped around the wrist, but few men adopted the habit of bracelet wearing. In 1675, when England's Charles II helped popularize the long waistcoat, men routinely placed their watches in waistcoat pockets, and the term "pocket watch" was coined.

While a spiral spring was first used for the mainspring around 1500, in 1675 a spiral balance spring found its way onto the balance to become what we now know as the hairspring, a step that greatly improved timekeeping accuracy. This also led to the introduction of a minute hand, although for many more years most watches still only featured one hand.

Dutchman Christiaan Huygens (1629–1695) is widely credited with two of the most important innovations for mechanical timekeepers: the pendulum (1656) and the balance spring (1675), oscillating systems that improved the performance of the escapement. Clocks with pendulums became accurate to one minute a day for the first time in history. (Alternate theories credit Galileo with inventing the pendulum clock — his son Vincenzio apparently helped Galileo manufacture an unsuccessful model, which Vincenzio subsequently destroyed in a feverish rage later in life.) But the smaller pocket watch was not yet accurate enough to be used as a true timekeeper; it was still something more than jewelry and less than a tool. It took the man generally considered to be the greatest watchmaker of all to change this.

Abraham-Louis Breguet (1747–1823) started making his own watches in 1780, and through many innovations and inventions, including the overcoil balance spring and shock resistance for balance pivots, created a watch that both kept time well and looked beautiful.

Breguet, born in Switzerland, did his best work in France; yet it was Switzerland that eventually became the capital of time. Protestant reformer John Calvin had forbidden Genevan craftsmen from making something as frivolous as jewelry, but did encourage the manufacture of the more practical watch. The craftsmen responded enthusiastically.

As highly as Breguet is regarded, he didn't invent in a vacuum: His work was indebted to that of Peter and Jacob Debaufre and Nicolas Facio (who invented jeweled bearings); George Graham (temperature compensation, deadbeat escapement, cylinder escapement); Thomas Mudge (lever escapement); and John Arnold and Thomas Earnshaw (chronometer escapement). And, of course, there was John Harrison (1693–1776), the Englishman who developed and built the world's first successful maritime clock, whose accuracy was precise enough to allow the determination of longitude over great distances.

——

JAQUES MOREL, GENEVA, LA CHASSE, c. 1690, silver, mechanical movement with alarm. This is an example of an early Swiss pocket watch with a single hand, incorporating Huygens's balance spring, invented in 1675.

By the early nineteenth century, a great many watch manufacturers had sprung up, creating a multitude of models for the aristocracy, as well as for those in certain bourgeois professions such as medicine and transportation, where timekeeping had become increasingly important. The watch was in the process of transforming from a luxury to a necessity.

The construction of a watch, however, was still laborious and time-consuming, which is why the innovations of 1839 were so important: Swiss engineers Georges-Auguste Leschot and Pierre Frederic Ingold created machinery that could make interchangeable watch parts, permanently altering what had been a handmade industry. (It was, however, the Americans rather than the Swiss who took the lead in manufacturing partially machine-made watches that were both accurate and relatively inexpensive.)

More innovations followed, including the invention of keyless winding and hand setting (both Jean Adrien Philippe and Jules-Louis Audemars, among others, are given credit for the development). Initially the change of mode from hand setting to winding was accomplished via an external lever, or key, but this lever was now unnecessary; nor did a metal case need to be opened constantly. The snap-on bezel was added, and the hinged back could now be snapped shut. The dust cap mutated into a small hinged cover fitted inside the back, and the movement was screwed in place instead of hinged. (*continued on page 16*)

Complications

Watches that do more than tell the time of day to the second are described as having "complications." Simple complications might include the date or the power reserve (that is, how much longer a watch will run before needing to be rewound). A chronograph is a complication that measures elapsed time to the second after a button is pressed. A moon indicator keeps track of the moon's phases.

Over time, watchmakers have invented different ways to display the data measured by a complication on a watch dial. Not all complex or unusual dial arrangements reflect complications. For example, watches with so-called regulator dials that use different registers or sub-dials to show hours, minutes, and seconds may appear very complex, but they are actually simple timekeepers.

Virtually all of the complications and dial arrangments used in modern wristwatches first made their appearance in pocket watches in the eighteenth and nineteenth centuries.

ABOVE LEFT: **HAAS NEVEUX & CO, GENEVA, TRIPLE COMPLICATION,** c. 1890, yellow gold, mechanical movement with perpetual calendar, split-seconds chronograph, minute-repeater, and moon-phase display.

ABOVE: **GUINAND, PARIS,** c. 1800, gold, mechanical movement with date. This unusual watch has a mechanism for showing the date in its large central aperture.

BREGUET CHRONOS-BREGUET, c. 1820, gold, mechanical movement. The digital watch is not a modern creation. Watchmakers have always played with interesting methods of displaying the slow-moving hours; this is called a wandering hour watch.

LE ROY & FILS, PARIS, THE TWO COCKERELS, c. 1830, gold, mechanical movement. This watch offers a digital readout of hours and minutes, combined with a conventional second hand. The hour in its own aperture is called a "jumping hour."

CUGNIER LESCHOT, GENEVA, THE STORY OF ZEUS, c. 1820, gold, mechanical movement with quarter repeater. A watch with a visible movement is called "skeletonized," which is not considered a complication.

RIGHT: **UNKNOWN MAKER, GENEVA, DAY AND NIGHT,** c. 1780, gold, mechanical movement with calendar, day/night display and moon-phase indicators. This watch has two faces: The day side is showing.

FAR RIGHT: **BREGUET RETROGRADE PERPÉTUEL,** c. 1870, gold, mechanical movement with perpetual calendar and moon-phase indicator. This watch, made for the Islamic market, has a retrograde date display.

FAR LEFT: **HENRI BOITEL, PARIS, EXPOSITION UNIVERSELLE DE 1867,** 1867, gold, mechanical movement with Réaumur thermometer. Wristwatches that measure the temperature are uncommon. Some high-tech contemporary dive watches measure water temperature.

LEFT: **JOHN POOLE, LONDON,** 1873–74, gold, mechanical movement with chronograph. This is an example of a regulator dial: Minutes, hours, and seconds are given in separate registers, with an additional second hand for the chronograph function.

With the introduction of the second hand, some makers provided one that could be stopped, for timing. However, in these early watches, stopping the second hand also stopped the entire watch. The first true chronograph was designed in 1844 by Adolphe Nicole; it wasn't until 1862 that the contemporary three-pusher system was used.

Another great innovator, Dresden-born Adolf Lange, was not only a superb watchmaker but was interested in fair labor practices. Thanks to him, the town of Glashütte in what is now eastern Germany turned into a center for watch manufacturing. Lange devised ways to make sure that his employees were well educated enough to form their own companies, each of which could continue to supply his firm with excellent parts. He also created the great brand that became A. Lange & Söhne.

The need for accurate timepieces was spurred by the industrial revolution. For the first time, more people worked in factories than at home, and they worked there for a specified amount of time; that period had to be recorded for proper payment. Employers and employees both wanted to keep track of this record, and both used timepieces, which soon proliferated.

And, of course, a new means of transportation was becoming common: the train. Trains work best when they operate on an invariable schedule, reducing the likelihood of accidents, as well as making it convenient for fare-paying passengers to leave at a set time. Watch companies started creating watches specifically for railroad engineers and conductors, and accuracy was more important than ever.

At the end of the eighteenth century, about four hundred thousand timepieces were being made annually; seventy-five years later, that number had increased approximately 500 percent.

But these were primarily pocket watches; the wristwatch was worn only by women, often as a fashion accessory. Men avoided it. Moreover, the established watchmaking community disdained wristwatches; and, due to their small size, few manufacturers believed they could be constructed with a serious degree of accuracy, nor made strong enough to endure the rigors of constant exposure on the wrist.

The tide started turning in the late nineteenth century, in large part because soldiers discovered the usefulness of the wristwatch during wartime. Pocket watches, which required at least one free hand to operate, were difficult to use in combat. Soldiers began fitting watches on leather straps tied around the wrist, freeing up the hands to operate weapons.

Breguet claims to have made a wristwatch for the Queen of Naples in 1810, and Patek Philippe says it made a wristwatch for the Countess Kocewicz in 1868, but Girard-Perregaux seems to have been the first brand to make wristwatches in any quantity for men — in 1886, the company equipped the German Imperial Navy. American manufacturers were also looking into the market. By the end of the century, the Waterbury Clock Company (which eventually became Timex) was selling a men's wristwatch (for $3.50). Other manufacturers explored the potential. In 1904, Omega bought an advertisement in a German newspaper describing the Boer War–related exploits of a British military officer, who reportedly stated that a wristwatch was a necessary part of combat equipment because it freed soldiers from having to dip into their pockets to check the time.

————

In 1906, the evolution of wristwatches took another step forward with the introduction of wire loops (or lugs) soldered on to small, open-faced pocket-watch cases, allowing leather straps to be more easily attached. Another concern was the vulnerability of the glass crystal, especially when worn during combat; the solution became a pierced metal cover placed over the dial, protecting the glass but still allowing the time to be read.

One of the next milestones came in 1907, when Brazilian aviator Alberto Santos-Dumont asked his friend, renowned jeweler Louis Cartier, to make a watch he wouldn't have to keep taking out of his pocket while navigating the plane. Cartier quickly created the Santos, with a movement provided by the watchmaker Jaeger (which was soon to merge with LeCoultre to create one of the giants of the watch industry).

World War I did more for the men's wristwatch than any other single event in the history of timepieces. Allied troops were routinely issued wristwatches, and their reliability and convenience won the loyalty of soldiers. When the war ended, the soldiers returned home where, accustomed to the convenience of the wristwatch, they refused to return to the pocket watch. The wristwatch could no longer be construed as feminine if it was favored by the Great War's military heroes.

Models were also created featuring lugs that were integrated into the design of the case, which gave the watch a more finished appearance. And to enhance the watch's durability, metal dials were beginning to replace porcelain ones, which had been susceptible to cracking and chipping. Similarly, fragile glass crystals were replaced with those made of newly invented synthetic plastics.

After the war, Louis Cartier created another classic — the Tank, made to resemble the tracks of another new invention: the armored tank. Cartier presented the watch to the American general John J. Pershing, commander of American troops in France. The watch, on the market in 1919, was one of the most emulated designs in watch history.

Acceptance among men was further solidified after a high-altitude flight record was set by a pilot wearing a wristwatch; athletes at the 1920 Olympics also wore them.

One company that found great success with these new wrist pieces was Wilsdorf & Davis, Ltd., later renamed the Rolex Watch Company. Hans Wilsdorf, the company's founder and director, was a strong proponent of wristwatches and worked obsessively to make them accurate and reliable. In 1927, a British secretary swam the English Channel wearing a Rolex wristwatch, proving it was waterproof; Wilsdorf had presented the swimmer with the watch, and also made sure photographers were present to record that it still worked after the crossing. The new brand was called the Oyster; it's still one of the company's most popular models.

CARTIER TANK AMERICAIN, platinum, mechanical movement. Cartier's Tank has appeared in many versions.

Rolex also popularized self-winding wristwatches after adopting a reliable automatic system designed by Englishman John Harwood.

Although watch-industry traditionalists still felt the pocket watch represented the future — and throughout the 1920s more of them were produced than wristwatches — by the end of the decade the wristwatch was outselling the pocket watch. Companies added many more wrist models to their catalogs; by the mid-1930s, wristwatches accounted for fully 65 percent of all watches exported by Switzerland.

Wristwatches had arrived. Increasingly accurate, water-resistant, and self-winding, they were worn in adventurous situations and were heavily publicized as such; in 1933 Admiral Byrd wore a wristwatch on his second expedition to the South Pole.

With the triumph of the wristwatch assured, new and more interesting models were created, such as Jaeger-LeCoultre's reversible Reverso, Vacheron Constantin's louvered Jalousie, and IWC's antimagnetic Mark X.

World War II interrupted the advance; many manufacturers either slowed or stopped production, although neutral Switzerland continued making watches for the military. But after the war, watchmaking flourished again. Fancy new models were produced, thinner movements invented, and more complications introduced, including chronographs, alarms, and moon-phase indicators.

By 1950, about forty million watches a year were being manufactured. (The number today is about three hundred million.)

For the most part, through the 1950s and 1960s, dial designs of the major watchmakers remained conservative, although some of the smaller manufacturers, and many American designers, started playing with some of the popular

new art forms, such as Op Art in the sixties. Outstanding new designs included the irregularly cased watches designed for Patek Philippe and Hamilton by Gilbert Albert and Richard Arbib, respectively. And, for Movado, Nathan George Horwitt came up with a face that was simple, clean, and used only one mark, a gold dot at the twelve o'clock position, along with hour and minute hands. Eventually known as the Museum Watch, as it was the first watch to be displayed in New York's Museum of Modern Art, it is still a mainstay of the Movado brand.

Still, there was little need to innovate or change the overall wristwatch concept; according to common wisdom, the mechanical wristwatch had triumphed.

The reality was different: The wristwatch was about to face a thorough upheaval.

———

In looking for new ways to power timepieces, as well as to ensure accuracy, technicians had begun experimenting with new electronic regulating devices, one of which was quartz. The first battery-operated quartz clock was produced in 1929 by a Canadian, Warren Morrison, at New Jersey's Bell Laboratories. Soon afterward quartz clocks became popular in places where precision was necessary, as the new technology kept time better than mechanical clocks.

Although battery-powered watches were being developed by the early 1950s, the electronic watch, which replaced the mechanical escapement with the electronic vibrations of a tuning fork, was not considered a threat to the mechanical watch. The former remained bulky, unattractive, and for the most part, ignored by consumers. Still, the Asian watch industry saw possibilities in the new technology — particularly the Japanese, who had never found the means to compete with the Swiss. Now they began exploring ways to mass-produce inexpensive, accurate quartz watches. They couldn't beat the Swiss at the Swiss's game, but they suspected that if they invented new rules, they could prosper.

In the meantime, the American Hamilton brand was introducing its own line of battery-operated watches, especially for its Richard Arbib–designed space-age models, the Ventura and the Pacer. These were enormously successful. (Swatch, which now owns Hamilton, has reissued both.)

To compete with Hamilton, in 1960 Bulova came out with its own version of a battery-powered watch, the Accutron, featuring a tuning-fork regulator. Throughout the 1960s this very successful watch looked as though it might replace the mechanical watch, and other companies began developing similar models.

But the electric watch wasn't the future. Quartz was. Although the Swiss were working on quartz models, the Japanese companies Seiko and Citizen beat them to the market with quartz watches that offered consumers something new: extremely reliable timepieces that cost a fraction of the price of a mechanical watch. By 1969, Seiko had introduced its first line of quartz watches, the SQ Astron. It sold more units than any watch-industry expert had predicted.

What horologists now refer to as the quartz revolution horrified the Swiss industry. It also changed the business forever. Hundreds of good companies disappeared. Reputable brands such as Jules Jürgensen, Angelus, Büren, Enicar, and Record were never heard from again. In 1969, there were about sixteen hundred watch companies in Switzerland; today, there are approximately 650 (and some of these appeared only after the mechanical revival of the 1980s).

Other brands feared for their futures and searched out new sources of capital, often unsuccessfully, or were sold to those who at the time seemed dubious buyers of companies whose stock-in-trade — creating mechanical watches — appeared to have lost all its promise.

Still other brands attempted to manufacture quartz watches of their own, but most failed to see the potential of mass production and produced expensive models that couldn't compete with the Japanese. Other companies experimented with varying forms; for example, in 1970, following the success of its electric watches, Hamilton brought out the Pulsar, a quartz model with a digital LED (light-emitting diode). These ungainly watches were interesting but burdened with flaws — the batteries expired quickly and the display was difficult to read. Eventually, LED gave way to the LCD (liquid-crystal display), which created a constant display, but by then it was too late for Hamilton.

———

The mechanical watch reached its nadir in the 1970s. There was talk that the Swiss watch industry would never recover. Anxiety and unemployment gripped the Swiss valleys where watchmaking had been entrenched for centuries.

Then came two unexpected developments. First, in 1983, the Swiss introduced a line of inexpensive and well-designed quartz watches: the Swatch. The Swatch sold for as little as $35, because it had far fewer parts than a normal mechanical watch. And yet, it was a Swiss watch, with Swiss design, and Swiss reputation behind it. Swatch sold tens of millions of watches within a few years of its inception; the models were so well-designed, and so well-marketed, that they even became collectors' items when issued in limited numbers. The quartz revolution was no longer quite as frightening to the Swiss now that one of their own was taking the lead.

The other development may have been a psychological reaction to the rapid changes taking place. The quartz watch was a stunning success, but perhaps because of the need to counterbalance technology with humanism, the notion of the handmade, mechanical watch was reborn. Not every consumer wanted a sturdy quartz watch. Some wanted something only the mechanical watch could offer: a small piece of hand-tooled technology that fascinated by virtue of its intricacy. And, there was the prestige factor: Someone who could afford a ten-thousand-dollar watch wanted exactly that, a timepiece that displayed not just superior technology but cachet as well.

Just a decade after the panic had set in, firms that had almost disappeared saw a resurgence in orders, and new companies were emerging to take advantage of this high-end interest. They quickly found consumers who yearned for mechanical watches, extra complications, and dials that harkened back to the past.

These changes took place at a time when the world economy was booming, and the luxury markets in cars, fashion, and other areas were flourishing; watches were only part of this expansion.

The booming world economy helped spur another surprising development: the interest in vintage watches. In the 1980s, wristwatches rather than pocket watches became the mainstay of auctions and jewelers; houses such as Christie's and Sotheby's were holding auctions that featured wristwatches, while Italian watchmaker Osvaldo Patrizzi founded the auction house Antiquorum, which now sells far more watches at auction than any other company.

Similarly, starting in the 1990s, watches both new and pre-owned became an essential part of online trading. On any given day on eBay, as many as seventy-five thousand watches are for sale. Most stores now have online outlets, and some retailers exist only on the Internet.

Meanwhile, watches themselves grew increasingly complicated. In the early 1990s, IWC debuted its Il Destriero Scafusia, at the time the world's most complex wristwatch, with twenty-one different functions, including a tourbillon, perpetual calendar, and a minute repeater. It was soon

BELOW LEFT: **PATEK PHILIPPE CALATRAVA**, early 1940s, yellow gold, mechanical movement. The Calatrava became the classic midcentury men's dress watch.

BELOW: **VACHERON CONSTANTIN JALOUSIE**, 1990s, rose gold, mechanical movement. Vacheron & Constantin, as it was then called, created this design in the 1930s.

A BRIEF HISTORY OF TIMEPIECES

eclipsed by models from companies such as Patek Philippe and Gérald Genta.

Gérald Genta, the man, was another new phenomenon. A Swiss designer who had created the first stainless steel sports watch for Audemars Piguet (the Royal Oak), as well as the Nautilus for Patek Philippe and many other iconic pieces, Genta founded his own eponymous brand, which flourished, and then was sold to Bulgari. Meanwhile, designer Daniel Roth, who helped create Breguet's new image, started a company to produce watches with a distinctive ellipto-curvex shape (also now owned by Bulgari). Soon numerous eponymous brands sprang up — Roger Dubuis, whose extra-large watches helped set a trend; F. P. Journe, whose beautifully crafted dials make him one of the most award winning of all watchmakers; and Franck Muller, whose stunning watches compete with Patek Philippe, Audemars Piguet, and Vacheron Constantin for customers.

Other brands were offered by watchmakers such as the Dane Svend Andersen, the Italian Michel Parmigiani, the Frenchman Alain Silberstein, and the Germans Rainer Brand and Rainer Nienaber. New companies were formed to take advantage of the mechanical boom, including Chronoswiss, with its signature regulateur dials; Dubey & Schaldenbrand, one of the few companies run by a woman, as well as Maurice Lacroix, Paul Picot, Sothis, and Xemex, and many others.

Some companies were revived. Blancpain, which had fallen into desuetude, soon became a leader in luxury watches. Glashütte, once a prominent East German company that was folded into a large conglomerate, was resuscitated after the Iron Curtain fell, as was its sister brand, A. Lange & Söhne, now one of most prestigious of all. Ulysse Nardin is once again alive, with its intricately complicated watches.

And veteran companies such as Jaeger-LeCoultre and Girard-Perregaux, which throughout the twentieth century sold solid mid-level watches, were now producing high-end, complicated ones. Zenith, for years forbidden from selling in the American market due to its shared name with the American electronics concern, also transformed into a worldwide brand.

———

With the economy in its favor, the watch business shook off its 1970s doldrums. For decades, one year after another didn't bring much variety. Today, the industry more closely emulates the car business — each year, new models are brought out and older ones retired. And whereas for centuries the trend was to create the smallest movement possible (and thus the thinnest watches), around the turn of the twenty-first century huge, oversize watches became popular, and a company like Vacheron Constantin, which once sold watches as thin as five millimeters, was, like its rivals, now selling ones three times as thick.

In 2004, imports of Swiss watches to the United States set a sales record at $1.62 billion. (After the United States, the next biggest markets for Swiss watches are Hong Kong, Japan, and Italy.) Advertising expenditures are high — Rolex alone spent $38.2 million in 2004 (Movado was second, at $13.59 million; Citizen third).

Today, watch lovers can satiate their needs through any number of avenues. Watch magazines such as *WatchTime* and *International Watch* help both novices and collectors sort out models. The Internet has become a source for almost everything anyone could want to know about the subject, and sites such as ThePuristS.com, TimeZone.com, and EquationofTime.com have hugely devoted followings: Watch companies all have sites as well, as do the top watch retailers.

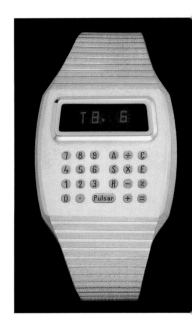

HAMILTON PULSAR FOR TIFFANY, 1970s, gold, quartz movement with LED display

PAUL PICOT FIRSHIRE 3000, 2000s, stainless steel, self-winding mechanical movement with date and power-reserve indicator. Numerous contemporary watches employ variations of the regulator dial.

ALAIN SILBERSTEIN KRONO 2, c. 1994, PVD-coated steel, self-winding mechanical movement with chronograph, date, and moon-phase indicator. Silberstein's whimsical designs show the intersection of haute horology with the world of designer watches.

Once again, however, clouds loom on the horizon. Some people now use their cell phones as watches; they are accurate and handy. We live at the dawn of the high-tech age. Technology still has a long way to go, and one place where it will travel is to the wrist — soon we may be able to wear small wrist-computers that not only tell time but make phone calls, take messages, snap pictures, and show movies, as well as perform other functions that we haven't yet considered. How will a simple watch compete?

Just as the beginnings of timekeeping are unknown, so is its future. As of now, however, the mechanical watch is thriving. Even if the modern computer can be set into a wrist-sized format, there's still room for a mechanical wonder on the other wrist. Or perhaps fashion will evolve again, and mechanical watches will return to the pocket, or around the neck. Another possibility: They may mate with the computer to produce a sort of electro-mechanical hybrid. Assuming the mechanical watch business learned a lesson from the quartz revolution, the next time a peril appears, watchmakers will be prepared to address it.

Over the centuries, the tools of timekeeping have moved from the largest objects in the sky to what is probably the smallest piece of mechanical technology. The need to measure and know time is part of human nature. If for some reason the wristwatch, like the sundial and hourglass, disappears, it will be replaced by something equally inventive and equally capable of helping us know exactly what time it is every second of the day.

RIGHT: **GÉRALD GENTA RÉTRO SOLO**, c. 2000, stainless steel, self-winding mechanical movement. Genta's designs have strongly influenced the contemporary interest in features like jumping hours.

FAR RIGHT: **A. LANGE & SÖHNE LANGE 1**, 2000s, white gold, mechanical movement with date and power-reserve indicator. The Lange 1, with its sub-dials and large-date window, was one of the most influential designs of the mechanical watch revival. It is the quintessential modern dress watch.

FIFTY BRANDS

PATEK PHILIPPE REF. 130,
1938, stainless steel, mechanical movement with chronograph

A discussion among aficionados about watch brands almost always leads to an argument. Few collectors feel as passionately and personally about their choices. If you ask twenty of them to list the top twenty brands, you'd get twenty different opinions and as many full-fledged debates as well.

Watch collectors talk about brands the way others gossip about people. Get those twenty enthusiasts into one room, and they'll chat as though the brands were personal friends or enemies. "Brand X just fired a pal of mine, so I'll never buy anything that company makes." "Brand Y's new movement is cheap, so avoid everything the brand's ever done." "Brand Z's design is great — I love everything the company does."

All enthusiasts tend to be enthusiastic, no matter the object of their passion, but there is still something remarkable about grown men fighting passionately over a small, seventy-five-year-old piece of machinery. Check out one of the online watch forums listed in the back of this book if you want to observe the phenomenon firsthand. Like a perpetual-motion machine, it never stops.

That said, at the moment there are nearly a thousand companies that produce watches (still a far cry from the many thousands that existed before the quartz revolution). Selecting which fifty to profile is bound to create another argument. There isn't room in this book to discuss all the many brands that currently or used to exist — nor is there any need to, as most people interested in watches won't encounter them. So here are the facts on what could best be considered Fifty Brands You Should Know About.

The omissions will probably raise more hackles than the inclusions. Certainly, cases may be argued for the German watches of Rainer Brand, Rainer Nienaber, and Jörg Schauer (who not only makes interesting watches under his own name, but also owns the venerated brand Stowa), or for the Italian brands Anonimo and Carlo Ferrara (whose signature is a face with two dials that resemble racetracks, one for the hours and one for the minutes).

Likewise, Sothis, Davosa, Minerva, and Tutima all make reliable and interesting timepieces. Maurice LaCroix and Paul Picot are close to joining the top tier, and every year their watches get better. Doxa and Mido are brands with great histories, while de Grisogono and Bedat & Co are new brands determined to create history. Then there are the mid-level companies that year after year turn out reliable entry-level timepieces, such as Oris, Rado, Raymond Weil, Tissot, Xemex, and Swiss Army.

Another handful of brands are American, including Roland Murphy's RGM. This company is attempting to do the near-impossible: manufacture high-quality watches out of small-town America. Based in Mount Joy, Pennsylvania, RGM is just beginning to earn a reputation in the watch world, but it's still too early to call the brand's fate. Similarly, Kobold, out of Pittsburgh, produces a promising line of chronographs that resemble those of Sinn and Fortis; again, time will be the ultimate judge of the company's success.

The fifty brands included in this volume are those that are either important today, have historical significance, or are clearly up-and-coming. But as even these fifty top brands can be hard to keep straight, the following metaphor may help:

Think of an old European royal court. Patek Philippe is the king — stately, regal, and reserved. The king doesn't approve of fancy gimmicks or quick moves; he's solid, dependable — the top of the line.

Vacheron Constantin is the queen — flashy, sexy, and sometimes even startling. Audemars Piguet is the artist prince — bold, interesting, often more daring than others, always intriguing and often superb.

Jaeger-LeCoultre is the prime minister — shrewd, old, and reliable. Often behind the scenes, for years Jaeger-LeCoultre has been helping other companies survive thanks to its manufacturing know-how. Jaeger-LeCoultre doesn't have the largest and fanciest line, but what it does it does well and wisely.

Then there's Rolex, the knight — the strongest, most sturdy, and most trustworthy; Rolex will go into vigorous battle and come out none the worse for wear.

Breguet is the father of the king. Once the king himself, the company relinquished a leadership role many years ago. Today, however, Breguet has undergone a kind of radical plastic surgery and again is looking regal.

All the others are members of the court, but each serves a different role. A. Lange & Söhne is the young nobleman of distinguished heritage who may one day become king. Glashütte is Lange's lesser-known brother, who emulates him in many ways, and sometimes may even exceed him. Blancpain is the beautiful princess whose face causes others to swoon. Ventura and Nomos are the local artisans, working in small rooms off the castle to create little marvels Merlin might enjoy. Jaquet Droz is the dazzling newcomer, Hamilton the former rival to the king who has now married into the family, Elgin the long-lost American relative.

Here, then, are the members of the court of watches.

A. Lange & Söhne

Lange is a brand that is both rich in history yet in a sense brand-new.

The original company was established in 1868 in Glashütte, Saxony, by Adolf Lange (1815–1875) and his brother-in-law, Adolf Schneider, along with fifteen apprentices. Lange was a mechanical genius whose interest in machine tools propelled him to draw plans for innovative ways to manufacture watches. Following an apprenticeship to a famous clockmaker and keeper of the tower clock at the royal Saxon court in Dresden, he worked in Paris, England, and Switzerland. In 1842, after returning to Dresden, he married his former master's daughter and became co-owner of his father-in-law's business.

Lange was a man with a social conscience, and to invigorate the economically blighted area, he helped to create a watch *manufacture* in the nearby town of Glashütte, where he trained some of the local citizens in watchmaking skills. He soon steered his trainees into becoming specialists in manufacturing items such as screws, wheels, balance wheels, and hands. In so doing, Lange not only helped many become financially stable, but also was able to guarantee good relationships with local suppliers and thereby ensure freedom from dealing with more unpredictable foreign ones.

The firm quickly became well regarded for its beautiful pocket watches and eventually produced some stunning models, including a Grande Complication repeating pocket watch featuring a split-seconds chronograph, a perpetual calendar, and a moon-phase indicator.

When Lange died in 1875, his sons took over the business, now known as A. Lange & Söhne. And although World War I hurt the luxury watch market, the company survived due, in part, to its production of high-precision marine chronometers.

In 1919, Adolf's son Emil turned the company over to his own sons, who continued the Lange tradition. In 1930, Richard Lange patented a hairspring alloy that included the addition of beryllium, an important development in the evolution of the temperature-stable hairspring alloys in use today.

On May 8, 1945, Russian bombs destroyed Lange's main production building. It was soon rebuilt, but on March 18, 1946, the new East German government expropriated the company, having declared the three Langes now running the firm to be Nazis and therefore war criminals. The Lange family vehemently denied the charges. Walter Lange, Adolph's great-grandson, refused to work for the outfit that had taken over the company and was told that he had to mine uranium; instead, he fled into an American-occupied zone in Bavaria.

Shortly afterward, the Lange name ceased to exist on watches. It was now one of seven German companies organized into a combine under the name Glashütte Uhrenbetrieben, or GUB, by the Communist government.

When Germany was reunited in 1990, Walter Lange returned to Glashütte hoping to bring his family's company back to life. Four years later, with the financial backing of parent company LMH (Les Manufactures Horlogeres), the technical support of the other LMH brands (Jaeger-LeCoultre and IWC), as well as the marketing skills of revered IWC chief executive Günter Blümlein, Walter Lange was able to introduce the first line of Lange watches in a generation. The new models, including the Lange 1, the Saxonia, and the Arkade, were produced under the company name Lange Uhren GmbH.

The revived firm manufactures its movement components using modern computer-aided tools, but it decorates the movements by hand to a very high level of finish. Part of the charm of an A. Lange & Söhne timepiece is the experience of looking at the movement through the display back, where movement plates and bridges made exclusively of untreated German silver are revealed.

Richemont purchased LMH — and therefore Lange, IWC, and Jaeger-LeCoultre — in 2000. Today 345 employees work for Lange Uhren GmbH (45 percent of them watchmakers), producing a few thousand watches annually.

THIS PAGE: **A. LANGE & SÖHNE ANNIVERSARY LANGEMATIK** (front and back), 2000, platinum, self-winding mechanical movement

OPPOSITE TOP: **A. LANGE & SÖHNE DATOGRAPH** (front and back), 2000s, platinum, mechanical movement with chronograph and date

OPPOSITE BOTTOM: **A. LANGE & SÖHNE GROSSE LANGE 1** (front and back), 2000s, yellow gold, mechanical movement with date and power-reserve indicator

Lange is the poster child for the display back watch trend; these are watches that can be enjoyed from viewing either the watch's front or back.

FAR LEFT: **A. LANGE & SÖHNE POUR LE MÉRITE**, 1990s, yellow gold, mechanical movement with tourbillon and power-reserve indicator

ABOVE LEFT: **A. LANGE & SÖHNE DOUBLE SPLIT FLYBACK**, 2005, platinum, mechanical movement with split-seconds and split-minutes chronograph

A. LANGE & SÖHNE 1815 SIDESTEP, 2003, pink gold, mechanical movement

The Lange 1 is an important design not only for the company but for the industry in general, as it proved that well-thought-out, asymmetric designs could capture the imagination of the watch-buying public. When Gunther Blümlein ran Lange, his company also owned IWC and Jaeger LeCoultre. The big-date mechanism designed by JLC was exclusively reserved for Lange for a period of ten years, and helped establish the young brand, launching a trend that many other brands have since emulated.

A. LANGE & SÖHNE LANGE 1 TOURBILLON, 2000, pink gold, mechanical movement with tourbillon, date, and power-reserve indicator

A. LANGE & SÖHNE LANGE 1, c. 2000, platinum, mechanical movement with date and power-reserve indicator

FAR LEFT: **A. LANGE & SÖHNE LANGEMATIK-PERPETUAL**, 2001, platinum, self-winding mechanical movement with perpetual calendar and moon-phase indicator

LEFT: **A. LANGE & SÖHNE 1815 MOONPHASE**, 2000, pink gold, mechanical movement with moon-phase indicator

BELOW: **A. LANGE & SÖHNE CABARET MOONPHASE**, 2005, pink gold, mechanical movement with date and moon-phase indicator

On this spread are four distinct moon-phase complications. The Luna Mundi has the world's only synodic moon phase; it turns smoothly with the hour hand. The 1815 Moonphase is the world's most accurate moon phase. The Langematik-Perpetual has a moon phase precise to one day in 122 years. The Cabaret Moonphase has a simple moon phase accurate to one day in 2.3 years.

| A. LANGE & SÖHNE

A. LANGE & SÖHNE GRAND LANGE 1 LUNA MUNDI, 2003, white gold, mechanical movement with date, and power-reserve and moonphase indicators

Audemars Piguet

Jules-Louis Audemars (1851–1918) and Edward-Auguste Piguet (1853–1919) formed this company based in LeBrassus, Switzerland, in 1875. Both men were watchmakers, but Audemars ran the production end while Piguet handled sales. The new company had a slow start; the duo didn't register their name until 1882, and the firm's official founding took place seven years later.

Because the partners manufactured all of their own components and assembled their watches in-house, they were able to maintain strict quality control, and the company quickly became known for producing excellent high-end, complicated timepieces. But not many: Between 1894 and 1899, Audemars Piguet manufactured barely twelve hundred watches.

The founders' deaths did not stop Audemars Piguet from continuing its tradition of complex timepieces. And, exploiting its experience in miniaturizing pocket-watch functions, the company was quickly able to embrace wristwatches. By 1906, Audemars Piguet had produced a repeating wristwatch; in 1920, it introduced the world's smallest one. The company barely survived the Depression, but it recovered over the next decades, and by the 1950s was producing a highly successful line of excellent dress watches, including an ultra-thin model (the famous *nine-ligne* Calibre 2003) and chronographs.

In 1967, in cooperation with Jaeger-LeCoultre, Audemars Piguet set a new record for the thinnest automatic movement (2.45 millimeters). Three years later, it introduced the world's thinnest movement (3.05 millimeters) to include date display.

Then, in 1972, Audemars introduced the Royal Oak luxury sports watch. Named in honor of a trio of warships which, in turn, were named after a hollowed-out oak tree where King Charles II once hid to elude enemies, the Royal Oak was the first luxury sports watch to be made of stainless steel. Created by eminent watch designer Gérald Genta, it featured an octagonal shape (mimicking a ship's porthole) and prominent hexagonal screws.

The Royal Oak seemed like a huge risk when it was first introduced. Who was going to pay luxury prices for a steel sports watch? It turned out to be one of the smartest moves a watch company has ever made. The model, in continuous production ever since, now comes in many varieties and is said to account for well over half of Audemars's total sales. More than 150,000 have been sold.

In 1993 Audemars Piguet introduced the Royal Oak Offshore, a larger version of the Royal Oak with a variety of complications, including a chronograph, tachymeter, thirty-minute counter, twelve-hour counter, date display, seconds display, and automatic movement.

Audemars Piguet is still family owned — descendants of both the original Audemars and Piguets work at the company — and it maintains a register of every watch made and sold. One of the most well-respected of all brands, its line shows a great breadth of watches, from sports to dress watches, and from simple to enormously complicated.

The company's superb watchmakers and designers are constantly dreaming up new movements and complications. One of the reasons it can produce such wonderful complications is that it owns Renaud et Papi (now APR&P), perhaps the best of the complications specialists.

When the conglomerate Richemont bought Jaeger-LeCoultre, Audemars Piguet, which owned 40 percent of the latter, received a large influx of cash; it used the money to upgrade its research and development, as well as marketing.

ABOVE LEFT: **AUDEMARS PIGUET EXTRA-PLAT**, late 1940s, yellow gold, mechanical movement

ABOVE CENTER: **AUDEMARS PIGUET JUMP HOUR RÉPÉTITION MINUTES**, 1990s, yellow gold, mechanical movement with minute repeater

ABOVE RIGHT: **AUDEMARS PIGUET**, 1950s, pink gold, mechanical movement

RIGHT: **AUDEMARS PIGUET TOURBILLON AUTOMATIQUE**, 1986, yellow gold, self-winding mechanical movement with tourbillon. This is the first serially produced wristwatch tourbillon. Audemars also created some groundbreaking design features to make it thin: the watch's case is also the main plate of the movement.

Audemars's audacity and artistry in the high-complications realm is well exhibited by its Cabinet Series of limited-edition pieces — fewer than a half-dozen models have been produced. Watch aficionados sometimes refer to these highly complicated pieces as "complications cocktails" because they combine very-difficult-to-execute functions in a single piece.

AUDEMARS PIGUET MILLENARY, 1999, yellow gold, self-winding mechanical movement with date, second time zone, and power-reserve indicator

AUDEMARS PIGUET, 1990s, yellow gold, self-winding mechanical movement with chronograph and date

AUDEMARS PIGUET, late 1940s, yellow gold, mechanical movement with perpetual calendar and moon-phase indicator

ABOVE: **AUDEMARS PIGUET
MILLENARY STAR WHEEL**,
2000, yellow gold, self-winding
mechanical movement

RIGHT: **AUDEMARS PIGUET
MÉTROPOLIS**, 2000, platinum,
self-winding mechanical
movement with perpetual
calendar and world time

FAR LEFT: **AUDEMARS PIGUET ROYAL OAK DUAL TIME**, 1990s, stainless steel, self-winding mechanical movement with date, second time zone, and power-reserve indicator

LEFT: **AUDEMARS PIGUET ROYAL OAK DAY AND DATE**, c. 2000, yellow gold, self-winding mechanical movement with date and moon-phase indicator

BELOW: **AUDEMARS PIGUET ROYAL OAK QUANTIÈME PERPÉTUEL**, 1990s, stainless steel and gold, self-winding mechanical movement with perpetual calendar and moon-phase indicator

If any high-end brand is known for a singular iconic design, it's Audemars Piguet for the Royal Oak. Since 1972, the Royal Oak case has housed everything from ultra thins to sophisticated complications. The Royal Oak Offshore, launched in the early 1990s, helped start the craze for extra-large watches.

RIGHT: **AUDEMARS PIGUET ROYAL OAK**, c. 1990, stainless steel and gold, mechanical movement with date

AUDEMARS PIGUET

Bell & Ross

It sounds like an English or American company, but it's actually named for its Continental founders, Bruno Belamich and Carlo Rosillo. Only a little more than a decade old, Bell & Ross creates watches for professionals such as divers, pilots, or (according to the company brochures) bomb disposal experts, which doesn't seem like a large market. Its watches were originally produced by the German company Sinn; now Bell & Ross has its own production plant.

The French firm uses only Swiss movements, and its watches are all water-resistant and highly readable, with large dials and large numerals. Thanks, in part, to the lucidity and elegance of these dials, Bell & Ross has acquired a large fan base. It also makes some deceptively simple-looking multifunction quartz watches with a hidden LCD display housing various functions other than the time, all of which are activated through the crown.

Bell & Ross is best known for its chronographs, jumping-hour models, and the beautiful light beige-taupe color of its dials. Its newest model, the BR O1, is its flashiest — resembling an instrument clock, it offers the option of being worn on the wrist, taken off and used as a small clock, or placed on a pendant.

LEFT: **BELL & ROSS JUMPING HOUR,** 2000s, platinum, self-winding mechanical movement with power-reserve indicator

BELOW: **BELL & ROSS DOUBLE SUBDIAL JUMPING HOUR,** 2000s, platinum, self-winding mechanical movement with power-reserve indicator

BELL & ROSS DESERT TYPE 126XL, 2000s, stainless steel, self-winding mechanical movement with chronograph and date

FAR LEFT: **BELL & ROSS HYDROMAX 11000 M**, 2000s, stainless steel, quartz movement with date, water-resistant to 11,000 meters

LEFT: **BELL & ROSS AUTOMATIC CHRONOGRAPH**, c. 2000, titanium, self-winding mechanical movement with chronograph and date

RIGHT: **BELL & ROSS PILOT 10TH ANNIVERSARY**, 2000s, stainless steel, self-winding mechanical movement with chronograph and date

FAR RIGHT: **BELL & ROSS VINTAGE 120**, 2000s, yellow gold plate, quartz movement with split-seconds chronograph and date

BELL & ROSS VINTAGE 126,
2000s, stainless steel, self-
winding mechanical movement
with chronograph and date.
The rotor is custom made

BELL & ROSS BR 01-94
CHRONO, 2005, stainless
steel, self-winding mechanical
movement with chronograph
and date; water resistant to
100 meters

Blancpain

Like many highly renowned Swiss companies, the original Blancpain (which the company claims was founded in 1735), fell on hard times during the mid-twentieth century. The last member of the Blancpain family died in 1932; for decades afterward, Blancpain watches were produced by Rayville. Eventually, the company passed into the hands of SSIH, composed primarily of Omega and Tissot, which closed it down, despite the success of many of its models, including its excellent dive watches.

Blancpain was resurrected in 1983 by Jean-Claude Biver, an Omega executive, and Jacques Piguet, a scion of one of Switzerland's most distinguished watchmaking families.

Biver purchased an old farmhouse in Le Brassus and, with Piguet, started turning out highly crafted mechanical watches with simple round cases and automatic movements. Throughout the 1980s, the company grew in reputation and sales. In the early 1990s, Blancpain realized its ambitious goal of producing six masterpieces of watchmaking, each with a different complication: an ultra-slim movement, a moon-phase indicator, a split-seconds chronograph, a perpetual calendar, a minute repeater, and a tourbillon. Not long afterward came a single watch containing all six complications.

Blancpain's trademark is its moon-phase indicator, found on many of its models, and its beautiful gold casing. But it also makes technologically innovative watches, such as one of the world's smallest self-winding chronographs, the Quattro, which has a tourbillon, fly-back chronograph, split-seconds feature, and a perpetual calendar. The company is also proud of its claim that it has never made a quartz watch.

In keeping with tradition, Blancpain watchmakers do not work in an assembly line but build each watch from inception to completion; only about ten thousand watches per year are produced. The movements come from Frédéric Piguet, with which Blancpain shares a building.

In 1992, the Swatch group purchased Blancpain for approximately a thousand times the amount Biver had paid to buy the name a decade earlier. Biver has now left the company, but Blancpain can still count on a fierce army of loyalists.

BLANCPAIN LÉMAN FLYBACK, 2000s, stainless steel, self-winding mechanical movement with chronograph and date

LEFT: **BLANCPAIN VILLERET CHRONOGRAPHE RATTRAPANTE,** 2000s, platinum, self-winding mechanical movement with split-seconds chronograph and date

RIGHT: **BLANCPAIN LÉMAN RÉVEIL GMT,** 2000s, white gold, self-winding mechanical movement with chronograph, date, alarm, second time zone, and power-reserve indicator

The famous Fifty Fathoms was commissioned by two French navy officers, who specified such details as the revolving bezel, screw-down crown, and luminous materials. Jacques-Yves Cousteau was among the many fans of this watch, which became one of the most influential of all divers' timepieces. Fifty fathoms — 91.45 meters — was the maximum dive depth for a diver using the standard scuba equipment available in the early 1950s.

BLANCPAIN FIFTY FATHOMS MILSPEC 1, 1960s, stainless steel, self-winding mechanical movement; water resistant to 91.45 meters

BLANCPAIN FIFTIETH ANNIVERSARY FIFTY FATHOMS, 2003, stainless steel, self-winding mechanical movement with date; water resistant to 300 meters

BLANCPAIN FIFTY FATHOMS, 1953, stainless steel, self-winding mechanical movement; water resistant to 91.45 meters.

BLANCPAIN CHRONOGRAPH PERPETUAL CALENDAR, 1990s, yellow gold, self-winding mechanical movement with chronograph, perpetual calendar, and moon-phase indicator

BLANCPAIN CONCEPT 2100, 2001, pink gold half-hunter case, self-winding mechanical movement with triple-date calendar and moon-phase indicator

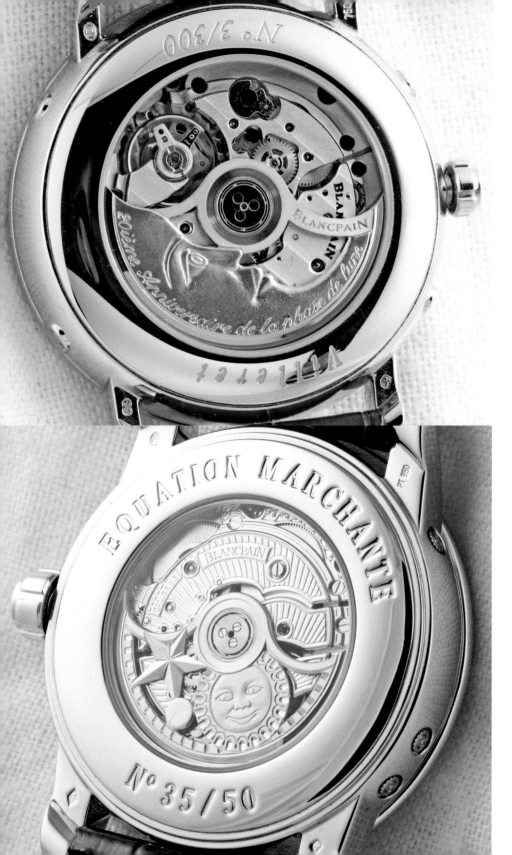

ABOVE: **BLANCPAIN LÉMAN** self-winding mechanical movement

TOP LEFT: **BLANCPAIN VILLERET 20IEME ANNIVERSAIRE DE LA PHASE DE LUNE** self-winding mechanical movement

LEFT: **BLANCPAIN VILLERET EQUATION MARCHANTE** self-winding mechanical movement. This is the back of the watch on the facing page

A good view of Blancpain's upgraded finishing style on its movements. Note the blued screws and engravings of the two watches above. On the Equation Marchante the screws and plates match. Blancpain recently announced that all its pieces will be made using the company's new one-watch-maker-per-watch manufacturing philosophy.

**BLANCPAIN PLATINUM
MASTERPIECE COLLECTION,**
1990s, boxed set of six watches

**BLANCPAIN VILLERET
EQUATION MARCHANTE,**
2000s, platinum, self-winding
movement with perpetual
calendar, equation of time,
running equation of time, and
power-reserve indicator

Breguet

If one person were to stand at the pinnacle of the pantheon of watchmakers, it would have to be Abraham-Louis Breguet (1747–1823).

When he was fifteen years old, Breguet moved from his native Switzerland to Paris, where he did most of his best work (although he did return to his home country during the tumultuous French Revolution).

Among other achievements, Breguet helped develop the automatic watch, originated the gong spring for a minute repeater (previous watches had sounded on a bell), invented the tourbillon, introduced critical advancements to the lever escapement, pioneered the use of the overcoil hairspring, designed one of the earliest shock protection devices, and helped create the keyless watch (at the time, watches were wound and adjusted by a key).

To this day, so many mechanisms and design features carry the Breguet name it's difficult to separate true inventions from inventive claims.

Breguet was also the watch world's first celebrity. A watch with a Breguet signature was worth a premium over others (part of the reason Breguet was the first watchmaker whose work was counterfeited). Writers from Alexandre Dumas to Jules Verne referred to Breguet in their novels; Marie Antoinette, Louis XVI, the tsar of Russia, the sultan of the Ottoman Empire, and the prince-regent of England all bought watches from him.

Breguet launched his firm in 1775, when his marriage to a wealthy woman gave him the means to open his own workshop. It was highly successful. When Abraham-Louis died, his son Antoine-Louis took over. In turn, Antoine's son, Louis-Clement, later ran the firm; Louis-Clement was a renowned scientist who eventually decided he preferred studying electricity to watchmaking and sold the company to Edward Brown, a Breguet workshop manager. (Louis-Clement Breguet's descendants went on to do pioneering work in the aeronautics industry.)

The Brown family owned Breguet until 1970, when Parisian jewelers Jacques and Pierre Chaumet bought the brand to give it new life; they sold the company to Investcorp in 1987. Today, it is owned by Swatch.

In the last few decades, Breguet watches have become renowned for their beautifully hand-engraved, silver-plate-over-gold dials and stunning cases with reeded edges; this style was updated from the originals and applied to the wristwatch by watchmaker and designer Daniel Roth.

Breguet also offers sportier models, such as the Type XX and Marine lines, but its dress watches are the company's best loved.

Swatch has recently invested in revitalizing the movement company Nouvelle Lemania; once an independent maker of movements closely associated with Breguet, it is now known as the Breguet Manufacture, meaning that Breguet can claim to create its own movements.

BREGUET HEURES SAUTANTES, 1990s, platinum, self-winding mechanical movement

ABOVE TOP: **BREGUET**, 1950s, yellow gold, mechanical movement

ABOVE BOTTOM: **BREGUET**, 1950s, yellow gold, mechanical movement

RIGHT: **BREGUET TYPE XX**,
1950s, stainless steel,
mechanical movement with
chronograph

FAR RIGHT: **BREGUET TYPE XX
AÉRONAVALE**, 1990s, platinum,
self-winding mechanical
movement with chronograph

**BREGUET MARINE CHRONO-
GRAPHE AUTOMATIQUE**,
1990s, platinum, self-winding
mechanical movement with
chronograph and date

BREGUET MARINE 5817PR
(unique piece), 2005, pink gold
and platinum, self-winding
mechanical movement with
date. This model usually comes
in stainless steel.

Many companies
supplied flyback chrono-
graphs to the military
during World War II, but
none are more collectible
than Breguet's Type XX.
The line was very successfully reintroduced in the
1990s, and it is hugely
popular, accounting for
as much as one-third of
the company's sales.
Breguet is trying to build
on its success by updating
its new luxury sports
model, the Marine,
with a larger, more mus-
cular, case.

49

Abraham-Louis Breguet is widely recognized as the greatest watchmaker who ever lived. The company he started, however, has had its share of ups and downs. In the 1970s and 1980s watchmaker Daniel Roth helped create its modern look. Roth's design concepts were influenced by Breguet pocket watches from the early nineteenth century; he adapted the coin-edge case, the signature Breguet hands, the solid-gold guillochet dial, and an array of classic complications associated with the founder.

BREGUET EQUATION OF TIME, c. 2000, platinum, self-winding mechanical movement with perpetual calendar, equation of time, and power-reserve indicator

BREGUET, 1990s, yellow gold, mechanical movement with moon-phase and power-reserve indicators

BREGUET SERPENTINE, 1990s, yellow gold, mechanical movement with triple-date calendar and moon-phase indicator

RIGHT: **BREGUET**, 1990s, yellow gold, mechanical movement

FAR RIGHT: **BREGUET**, 1990s, yellow gold, self-winding mechanical movement with perpetual calendar and moon-phase indicator

LEFT AND BELOW: **BREGUET TOURBILLON 1801–2001** (open and closed), 2001, white gold half-hunter case, mechanical movement with tourbillon

RIGHT: **BREGUET**, 1990s, yellow gold, mechanical movement with tourbillon, and power-reserve and retrograde twenty-four-hour indicators

RIGHT: **BREGUET TOURBILLON SQUELETTE**, late 1990s, white gold, mechanical movement with tourbillon

BREGUET FLYING-B TOURBILLON, 2000s, platinum, mechanical movement with tourbillon

Abraham-Louis Breguet created numerous timepieces with off-center dials and so does the modern company, especially for complications. Likewise, Breguet makes a wide range of tourbillons, as Breguet the man invented the device in 1801 to counteract the effects of gravity on the escapement.

BREGUET 1747–1997, 1997, platinum, mechanical movement with tourbillon, perpetual calendar, and minute repeater

Breitling

Founded in 1884 by Léon Breitling (1860–1914), this company built its reputation on aviation-themed timepieces such as cockpit clocks and pilots' watches. Its most famous model of the latter is the Navitimer, first introduced in 1952 and worn by pilots today.

The Navitimer is still being manufactured and now comes in many varieties, including the Aerospace, which features both analog hands and two digital displays. Another of the company's most famous models, from 1947, is the Chronomat — the first watch fitted with a circular slide-rule bezel.

The company's fame grew when, in 1962, astronaut Scott Carpenter wore his Breitling in space; in honor of this event, the model was dubbed the "Cosmonaute."

Like most Swiss companies, Breitling suffered greatly during the quartz era, but Sicura company executive Ernest Schneider bought it in 1979 and steered the firm into recovery. Today, it continues to sell solid chronographs and other complicated timepieces.

Two of its current lines are the Emergency (which can send out a radio signal if its owner is lost) and the Colt Superocean, which is waterproof to 100 ATM and COSC-rated. Breitling vintage watches tend to hold their value well.

TOP AND RIGHT: **BREITLING PREMIER** (dial and movement), 1940s, stainless steel, mechanical movement with chronograph

RIGHT: **BREITLING CHRONO-MAT**, 1940s, gold, mechanical movement with chronograph

FAR RIGHT: **BREITLING 1884 CROSSWIND CHRONOMETRE** (luminous dial), 2000s, stainless steel, self-winding mechanical movement with chronograph

BREITLING NAVITIMER, early
1960s, stainless steel, self-
winding mechanical movement
with chronograph

BREITLING EMERGENCY, late 1990s, titanium, quartz movement with chronograph, perpetual calendar, world time, alarm, and micro-antenna with aviation emergency frequency

FAR RIGHT: **BREITLING CHRONOMAT**, late 1940s, stainless steel, mechanical movement with chronograph, date, and moon-phase indicator

BREITLING YACHT TIMER,
1980s, stainless steel and gold,
self-winding mechanical
movement with chronograph
and date

BREITLING NAVITIMER QP,
1993, platinum, self-winding
mechanical movement with
chronograph, perpetual
calendar, and moon-phase
indicator

Bulgari

Bulgari, the world's third-largest jewelry producer after Cartier and Tiffany, has sold watches for many decades. Established over one hundred years ago in Rome by Greek silversmith Sotirio Bulgari (1857–1932), in 1977 the company hired Gérald Genta to design its own line of distinctive watches with a Bulgari look. Genta produced the Bulgari-Bulgari, featuring the company's name written twice on the bezel. Today the company is known for watches that are expensive and often contain intricate complications built on excellent movements.

Recently Bulgari, which in addition to selling jewelry has also expanded into everything from scarves to china, sunglasses, and leather goods, has strengthened its commitment to watches, buying both the Gérald Genta and Daniel Roth brands. This has led to new designs and suggests the company is establishing a serious footing in high-end timepieces.

BULGARI AUTOMATIC, 1999, stainless steel, self-winding mechanical movement with date

BULGARI ALUMINUM, 1990s, aluminum, self-winding mechanical movement with date

BULGARI SCUBA, c. 2000, stainless steel, self-winding mechanical movement with date; water-resistant to 200 meters

BULGARI AUTOMATIC, late 1990s, stainless steel, self-winding mechanical movement with chronograph

BULGARI ASSIOMA GRANDE COMPLICATION, 2006, platinum, self-winding mechanical movement with tourbillon, perpetual calendar, and two time zones

Bulova

Bulova was once one of the great American watch brands, but like many others, it stumbled badly. Joseph Bulova (1852–1935), its Bohemian-born founder, nonetheless created a company whose name is still among the most familiar in the business.

Starting as a small jewelry store on New York City's Maiden Lane, Bulova grew into a large watch and clock outfit; by 1931, it was running the watch industry's first million-dollar advertising campaign.

Using movements imported from Switzerland and cased in America, the company thrived, and Joseph's son Ardé took over the reins. During World War II, Bulova supplied the American government with military watches, specialized timepieces, aircraft instruments, critical torpedo mechanisms, and fuses.

More important to the history of watches, in the late 1940s the company started the Joseph Bulova Watchmaking School for veterans of World War II, graduating a large number of excellent watchmakers.

Ardé Bulova was an innovative thinker who became fascinated with the idea of a battery-powered watch. In the late 1950s, with the help of a Swiss engineer, the company developed the Accutron, an electronic watch with a tuning fork that is considered the forerunner to the quartz watch. The Accutron was an enormous success and came in many models, including the skeletonized Spaceview. (In the 1964 movie *Seven Days in May*, the camera pans in on a close-up of Kirk Douglas wearing a Bulova Accutron Astronaut.)

Perhaps because of the Accutron's success, the company was less enthusiastic about developing quartz watches (although it did eventually produce a quartz Accutron). As a result, the company foundered, and in 1979 it was taken over by the Loews Corporation. Today, the brand makes lower-end watches, although it is starting to create models to compete at higher price points. It also bought the old Wittnauer name and is relaunching the brand; Bulova owns the license for Harley-Davidson watches as well.

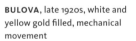

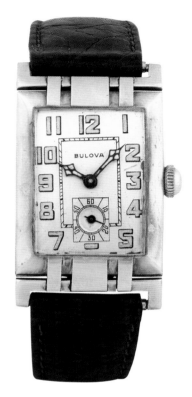

BULOVA, late 1920s, white and yellow gold filled, mechanical movement

BULOVA, late 1920s, white and yellow gold filled, mechanical movement

RIGHT: **BULOVA WRIST-ALARM**, 1953, yellow gold, mechanical movement with alarm

FAR RIGHT: **BULOVA**, 1960s, stainless steel, self-winding mechanical movement with date; water resistant to 200 meters

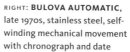

BULOVA ACCUTRON SPACEVIEW, 1965, yellow gold filled, electric movement

RIGHT: **BULOVA AUTOMATIC**, late 1970s, stainless steel, self-winding mechanical movement with chronograph and date

RIGHT: **BULOVA ACCUTRON ASTRONAUT**, 1964, stainless steel, electric movement with twenty-four-hour hand

Cartier

Unlike other major watch brands, Cartier is first and fore-most a jewelry company — and one of the world's most famous. Yet the company also can claim a significant history of watchmaking.

Cartier was founded in 1847 by Louis-François Cartier (1755–1793), a master goldsmith and jeweler who, like Abraham-Louis Breguet, became a favorite of the aristocracy. His particular patron was Princess Mathilde, the cousin of Napoleon III; he also sold the Empress Eugénie a silver tea service in 1859.

In the same year, Cartier set up shop in one of Paris's most fashionable neighborhoods, where the company thrived. In 1874, son Alfred Cartier (1841–1925) took over — but it was Alfred's son Louis (1875–1942) whose marketing skill transformed the business into an international success, with shops around the world.

The company had long made and sold pocket watches, but Louis Cartier, a great admirer of the mechanical watch, wanted his own line. Intrigued when Brazilian aviation pioneer Alberto Santos-Dumont (1873–1932) requested a watch he could use while flying, Cartier created the Santos model (1906), one of the first wristwatches designed specifically for men. Another influential design appeared in 1917, when Cartier introduced the Tank watch, fashioned in the shape of tank tracks. The Tank was in the forefront of the rectangular watch craze.

A few years later, Cartier formed a joint venture with Edward Jaeger to produce movements for Cartier (soon thereafter Jaeger joined the company LeCoultre to form Jaeger-LeCoultre). Cartier also used movements from Vacheron Constantin, Audemars Piguet, and Movado, the latter especially for the company's triple-date watches.

In the 1921 movie *The Sheik*, Rudolph Valentino wears a Cartier Tank; perhaps this is what inspired the widely circulated but apocryphal story that the later Cartier Pasha came about because the pasha of Marrakech requested a watch he could wear while swimming.

Louis Cartier died in 1942, and the company faltered. It was eventually broken into several smaller companies, but was rescued by a group of investors who from 1972 to 1979 re-unified the pieces into Cartier Monde SA. Then, in 1988, Cartier purchased 60 percent of Piaget (which owned Baume & Mercier); soon Cartier Monde was renamed the Vendôme Luxury Group (later called the Richemont group) when it merged with Dunhill's non-tobacco division.

Cartier sells its watches in its own retail shops, which seems to add cachet to the line — one doesn't just buy a Cartier watch, one buys the watch and a piece of the Cartier store's prestige.

Tiffany and Baume & Mercier

Unlike Cartier, Tiffany, founded in New York in 1837 by Charles Lewis Tiffany, elected to sell other brands in its stores, with the Tiffany name printed on the dial. Today Tiffany is more ambitious. Its best-known models are the Atlas (below), whose dials have no markings but whose bezels bear Roman numerals, and its Tiffany Mark line, which features designs derived from the pocket watches the store sold many decades ago. And for those who can't afford Cartier, consider its younger sister, Baume & Mercier, which is actually one of Switzerland's oldest brands, dating from 1834. Baume & Mercier manufactured many beautiful watches, particularly its mid-century chronographs, before slumping in the 1960s, but it is making good watches again today. Rival watchmaker Piaget bought a controlling interest in the firm in 1965. In 1988, Cartier purchased a majority interest in Piaget; today, all three brands are part of the Richemont empire.

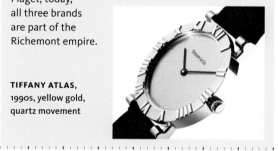

TIFFANY ATLAS,
1990s, yellow gold,
quartz movement

OPPOSITE TOP LEFT: **CARTIER TANK AMERICAIN**, 2000s, yellow gold, mechanical movement

OPPOSITE TOP RIGHT: **CARTIER TANK CINTRÉE DOUBLE FUSEAUX**, 2004, pink gold, two mechanical movements

OPPOSITE: **CARTIER TANK DIVAN**, 2000s, stainless steel, self-winding mechanical movement

ABOVE RIGHT: **CARTIER SANTOS 100**, 2004, stainless steel, self-winding mechanical movement

RIGHT: **CARTIER SANTOS GALBÉE**, 2003, stainless steel, self-winding mechanical movement

**CARTIER CARRÉ OR
SAVONETTE**, 1957, yellow gold
with sapphires, mechanical
movement

CARTIER VENDÔME B-PLAN,
1990s, white gold, mechanical
movement

ABOVE LEFT TO RIGHT:

CARTIER CEINTURE AUTOMATIQUE, 1972, yellow gold, self-winding mechanical movement

CARTIER GONDOLE, made c. 1975 for the sultana of Oman, yellow gold, mechanical movement

CARTIER VENDÔME AUTOMATIQUE, 1980s, white gold, self-winding mechanical movement

CARTIER MONETA, 1946, yellow gold, mechanical movement

RIGHT: **CARTIER TANK BASCULANTE**, 1990s, stainless steel, mechanical movement

Even people who consider Cartier more of a jewelry than a watch brand have to respect the company's remarkable success over the years. Many of horology's most influential designs spring from this manufacture, and Cartier continues to innovate in its Collection Privée, a high-end line of watches with interesting complications and design elements based on its Pashas, Tortues, and other models.

LEFT: **CARTIER TORTUE MONO POUSSOIR,** 2000s, yellow gold, mechanical movement with chronograph

RIGHT: **CARTIER COLLECTION PRIVÉE TORTUE,** 2004, platinum, self-winding mechanical movement with perpetual calendar and second time zone

Chopard

Better known today for its jewelry than its watches, Chopard was founded in 1860 by Louis-Ulysse Chopard (1836–1915) and made excellent pocket watches that were long favored by railroad employees; the company was also famous for its jewelry-studded timepieces. But in the 1960s it needed help staying afloat, so the Scheufele family of Pforzheim, Germany, with a background in jewelry and timepieces, took the helm, and still run it today.

Many of Chopard's watches borrow from the aesthetic of the company's jewelry lines and are highly decorated with diamonds and other precious stones; Happy Sport, one of its successful lines for women, features loose diamonds between the crystal and the dial.

Recently Chopard started making its own movements and asked famed watchmaker Michel Parmigiani to assist; today the well-regarded Chopard's L.U.C. movement (named in honor of the company's founder) is used in the company's most successful models.

Chopard also has a long history of good works: It has teamed with tenor José Carreras, who suffers from leukemia, in support of the Carreras Foundation, which funds research to fight the disease, and assists rock star Elton John's AIDS Foundation with a line of watches whose profits support the its work.

OPPOSITE: **CHOPARD MILLE MIGLIA GMT ALFA ROMEO,** 2005, stainless steel, self-winding mechanical movement with chronograph, date, and second time zone

ABOVE: **CHOPARD CALENDRIER PERPÉTUEL RÉTROGRADE LUNA D'ORO,** 1990s, yellow gold, self-winding mechanical movement with perpetual calendar and moon-phase indicator

RIGHT: **CHOPARD MILLE MIGLIA 1988–1998,** 1998, stainless steel, self-winding mechanical movement with chronograph

CHOPARD MONACO HISTORIQUE, 1990s, platinum, self-winding mechanical movement with split-seconds chronograph

OPPOSITE TOP: **CHOPARD
L.U.C. 1.96** (front and back),
2000s, yellow gold, self-
winding mechanical movement
with date

CHOPARD L.U.C. QUATTRO
REGULATEUR, 2005, white
gold, mechanical movement
with second time zone and
power-reserve indicator

OPPOSITE BOTTOM: **CHOPARD
L.U.C. SPORT 2000** (front and
back), 2000, stainless steel,
self-winding mechanical
movement with date

Chronoswiss

Gerd-Rudiger Lang (b. 1943) founded this German company in 1983 after running a service branch for the Heuer-Leonidas company for many years. When Heuer-Leonidas closed, Lang was left with no job but a great many watch parts and movements. Soon he was creating new watches using old movements, and placing transparent windows in their backs so that his customers could view them. Thus Chronoswiss got its start, helping to launch the high-mech watch renaissance.

In 1988, the company began producing a regulator dial, which had been common for centuries in clocks; this is the dial in which the minute and hour hands run on separate circles on one face.

Today Chronoswiss produces approximately five thousand watches a year — all with mechanical Swiss movements — and has become one of the most successful of the younger companies; its trademark Régulateur has been imitated by many other brands, but Chronoswiss keeps coming up with new versions. Its Opus line of skeletonized chronographs, available in steel, gold, and platinum cases, has also become a classic.

Chronoswiss has been particularly popular in its native Germany, but it is now selling internationally and finding a market in the United States; its watches are priced below most high-end brands and thus make an attractive entry-level purchase (although the company also produces some high-end watches, including a tourbillon).

FAR LEFT: **CHRONOSWISS RÉGULATEUR**, 1990s, gold, self-winding mechanical movement

LEFT: **CHRONOSWISS OPUS**, 1996, red gold, self-winding mechanical movement with chronograph and date

BELOW AND RIGHT: **CHRONO-SWISS DELPHIS**, c. 2000, pink gold and stainless steel, self-winding mechanical movement

To celebrate its twentieth anniversary, Chronoswiss commissioned Andreas Strehler, one of the youngest and most innovative members of the AHCI, to design the Chronoscope, a single-button chronograph with a regulator dial.

CHRONOSWISS CHRONO-SCOPE, 2003, gold, self-winding mechanical movement with chronograph

CHRONOSWISS DIGITEUR, 2005, platinum, mechanical movement with digital display

Citizen

The Japanese company Citizen is the world's largest watch-maker. Founded in Tokyo after World War I, the brand was so named to evoke the image of a company whose products can be bought by anyone, anywhere, for a good price, at a time when watches were still luxury items in Japan. Unlike the Swiss companies that faced extinction during the quartz revolution, by the mid-1970s Citizen was producing vast numbers of well-made quartz watches and winning many awards for innovation in their design and manufacture. The company's movements come from a subsidiary, Miyota, and are produced in enormous numbers and variations.

Citizen has created the world's smallest quartz movement, a light-powered movement (the Eco-Drive), and a radio-powered movement; it leads the world in special-function timepieces such as the Aqualand.

Citizen watches are not widely collected outside of Asia; they are, however, extremely popular as reliable, inexpensive timepieces. For the present, it also boasts the most accurate (non-radio-controlled) wristwatch in the world: The Citizen. A perpetual calendar, it is guaranteed accurate to five seconds per year. Citizen recently introduced high-end quartz watches featuring grand complications with various astronomical displays in its Campanola line.

LEFT: **CITIZEN AQUALAND 20TH ANNIVERSARY MODEL**, 2006, stainless steel, Eco-Drive movement with depth display, dive log, alarm, calendar, and two time zones; water resistant to 200 meters

FAR LEFT: **CITIZEN CAMPAGNOLA**, 2000, stainless steel, quartz movement with perpetual calendar

LEFT: **CITIZEN QUARTZ CYSTRON SOLAR CELL**, 1976, stainless steel, quartz movement with date

CITIZEN CYSTRON MEGA QUARTZ, 1975, gold, quartz movement with day and date. This watch tested accurate to ± 3 seconds per year

ABOVE: **CITIZEN CHRONO-MASTER THE CITIZEN**, 1995, yellow gold, quartz movement with date; guaranteed accurate to ± 5 seconds per year

LEFT: **CITIZEN QUARTZ EXCEED GOLD**, 1978, gold, quartz movement; thinner than 1mm

Corum

Since Corum's inception in 1955, its designs have helped it stand out from the competition. Known for its Admiral's Cup line of timers, often paired with tide displays, the company has also achieved recognition for its mechanical watches set inside gold coins, using guilders, pesos, and, above all, the United States twenty-dollar Liberty Eagle coin.

The coin watch is made by cutting the coin in half and carving out space for a small mechanical movement, which is then inserted inside. Most of these watches have lugs attached so the watch can be worn on a band or bracelet; others remain strapless and resemble a simple gold coin, but are equipped with a catch by the three o'clock position that opens the coin to reveal a small timepiece.

Corum has also recently launched a line of bubble-shaped crystals that rise almost twenty millimeters from the wrist, making them resemble little popcorn machines.

Perhaps Corum's most identifiable high-end watch is the Golden Bridge, in which the movement is suspended in a crystal, with the barrel, the entire wheel train, escapement, and balance arranged in one line. Designed by Vincent Calabrese (b. 1943), it is probably the Corum watch most sought by collectors and has recently been reintroduced.

The company has undergone several changes in ownership, and today is run by American businessman and watch lover Severin Wunderman, credited with building the Gucci watch brand.

LEFT: **CORUM ADMIRAL'S CUP ANNIVERSARY EDITION,** 1990s, pink gold, self-winding mechanical movement with quarter repeater and concealed automata

FAR LEFT: **CORUM GOLDEN BOOK THE MAGIC FLUTE,** 1996, pink gold, mechanical movement

LEFT: **CORUM ROLLS ROYCE,** 1980s, yellow gold, mechanical movement

OPPOSITE, CLOCKWISE FROM TOP LEFT:

CORUM BUBBLE CHRONO-GRAPH, 2000s, stainless steel, self-winding mechanical movement with chronograph

CORUM GOLDEN BRIDGE, 2000s, rose gold, mechanical movement

CORUM COIN WATCH, 200s, cased in United States twenty-dollar gold coin, self-winding mechanical movement

Daniel Roth

Watchmaker-turned-company-founder Daniel Roth (b. 1945) created a brand in which all the watches have the same shape: The company today calls it an ellipsocurvex — it looks like an oval crossed with an octagon.

A Frenchman, Roth first became famous in the watch world by helping Audemars Piguet create its ultra-slim movements. He then worked for the French jewelry company Chaumet, which had recently bought Breguet, and helped it relaunch the latter company by designing some of the most beautiful dials in horological history.

In the late 1980s, Roth went off on his own to create equally beautiful dials with movements supplied by leading manufacturers. The watches are also beautifully made and expensive. The Daniel Roth brand is now owned by Bulgari, and Roth himself is no longer part of his eponymous brand. Instead he is producing a small number of meticulously crafted pieces a year under the name Jean Daniel Nicholas.

DANIEL ROTH, 1990s, yellow gold, self-winding mechanical movement with date

DANIEL ROTH PERPETUAL CALENDAR, 1990s, yellow gold, self-winding mechanical movement with perpetual calendar

ABOVE: **DANIEL ROTH ATHYS**, 2000s, red gold, mechanical movement

ABOVE RIGHT: **DANIEL ROTH PERPETUAL CALENDAR MOON PHASES**, 2000s, platinum, self-winding mechanical movement with perpetual calendar and moon-phase indicator

RIGHT: **DANIEL ROTH RÉGULATEUR TOURBILLON DOUBLE FACE**, 1990s, pink gold, mechanical movement with tourbillon, and power-reserve and one-minute tourbillon indicators on the reverse side

FAR RIGHT: **DANIEL ROTH RÉGULATEUR TOURBILLON DOUBLE FACE** (back), 1990s, yellow gold

DANIEL ROTH PAPILLON, 2000s, platinum, self-winding mechanical movement

DANIEL ROTH METRO-POLITAN, c. 2000, stainless steel, self-winding mechanical movement with second time zone and day/night indicator

Dubey & Schaldenbrand

This company was founded in 1946 when the Swiss-born Georges Dubey, a watchmaking teacher, formed a partnership with fellow countryman and watchmaker René Schaldenbrand to create a very specific watch: a relatively inexpensive split-seconds, or *rattrapante*, chronograph; in this company's case, it was called an Index Mobile, and was the simplest design anyone had ever invented for such a device.

In the mid-1990s the company was sold to Cinette Robert, a descendent of two great Swiss horological families — the Meylans and the Jaeger-LeCoultres — who is today one of the few women to run a watch company. Robert was already a watchmaker and collector; she used her stash of approximately six-thousand vintage movements to create new Dubey & Schaldenbrand models in limited editions.

Today the watchmaker creates fewer than five thousand watches a year and has a small but devoted following, and some of the higher-priced models are beginning to turn up at auctions. Among its bestselling models are the Aerodyn and the Gran' Chrono. Dubey & Schaldenbrand also sells a full line of women's watches.

DUBEY & SCHALDENBRAND GRAN' CHRONO ASTRO, rose gold, self-winding mechanical movement with chronograph, triple-date calendar, and moon-phase indicator

DUBEY & SCHALDENBRAND AERODYN ELEGANCE, 2003, stainless steel, self-winding mechanical movement with date

DUBEY & SCHALDENBRAND GRAN' CHRONO, rose gold, self-winding mechanical movement with chronograph and date

DUBEY & SCHALDENBRAND AERODYN JUMPING HOUR, 2001, rose gold, self-winding mechanical movement

DUBEY & SCHALDENBRAND AEROCHRONO, 2003, stainless steel, self-winding mechanical movement with chronograph and date

DUBEY & SCHALDENBRAND GRAN' CHRONO ASTRO movement

DUBEY & SCHALDENBRAND SPIRAL SPLIT-SECOND, 2003, stainless steel, self-winding mechanical movement with split-seconds chronograph and date. The spring on the face of this model is decorative

RIGHT: **DUBEY & SCHALDEN-BRAND INDEX MOBILE**, 1990s, rose-gold plated, self-winding mechanical movement with split-seconds chronograph

FAR LEFT: **DUBEY & SCHALDEN-BRAND SPIRAL ONE**, 2002, rose gold, self-winding mechanical movement with chronograph and date

LEFT: **DUBEY & SCHALDEN-BRAND SPIRAL ONE** gold movement

The Index Mobile was one of the most creative approaches to the splits-seconds complication, which is one of the most difficult to execute. Dubey & Schaldenbrand came up with a hairspring on the dial connecting to the two second hands, as opposed to an elaborate mechanism deep inside the movement.

Dunhill

The English retailer Dunhill, best known for its luxury line of men's accessories, was founded by Alfred Dunhill (1872–1959) in 1893 as Dunhill Motorities.

Although still better known for its automobile- and tobacco-related products, the company produced pocket watches as early as 1906, and was known for combining watches with other accessories. These novelties included the watch-lighter, the watch-belt, and the watch-pencil, all dating from the early part of the twentieth century.

The company began making wristwatches in 1929 and sold them only at Dunhill stores. All parts came from Switzerland, except the straps, and that tradition continues.

A division of Richemont, Dunhill is now producing new designs that are much more daring and provocative than anything the company has done in the past. Yet its facet watch is one of the few that has been produced continuously since the 1930s.

In addition the company continues to make lighters, pens, and other goods.

DUNHILL A-CENTRIC PENTAGRAPH, 2006, stainless steel, self-winding mechanical movement with date and second time zone

DUNHILL WHEEL WATCH CHRONOGRAPH, 2006, stainless steel, self-winding mechanical movement with chronograph

Hermès and Montblanc

Other companies better known for non-watch wares are also trying to make a name for themselves with timepieces, including Hermès, the French luxury-goods brand that has been making elegant watches for many years, and Montblanc (right), best known for its line of expensive pens, which is now offering an impressive range of quartz and mechanical watches.

MONTBLANC TIMEWALKER, c. 2004, stainless steel, self-winding mechanical movement with date

LEFT: **DUNHILL UNIQUE A WATCH LIGHTER,** 1927, black-lacquered silver, mechanical movement

OPPOSITE: **DUNHILL WHEEL WATCH PETROLHEAD,** 2005, stainless steel, self-winding mechanical movement with date and power-reserve indicator

Eberhard

Founded by Georges-Émile Eberhard in 1887, Eberhard has long been a timekeeper for sporting events, especially car races, but also for aviation and navigation. In 1919, it introduced its first chronograph wristwatch. Five years later, it brought out its chronograph with two push-buttons, and in 1939 it launched a chronograph rattrapante. In the 1930s, the brand was the official supplier to the Italian Navy.

A favorite among those looking for reasonably priced, well-made watches, the company offers a nicely designed line with models ranging from the remarkably modern-yet-old-fashioned look of its eight-day power supply stainless steel watch to the striking Chrono 4, a chronograph with four smaller dials lined up straight across the bottom of the main dial. A new model has the four dials lining up vertically on one side.

As with Chronoswiss and Dubey & Schaldenbrand, purchasing an Eberhard can be an excellent, relatively inexpensive way to own a fine Swiss watch.

EBERHARD & CO.
MULTI-SCALE, 1940s, stainless steel, mechanical movement with chronograph

EBERHARD & CO.
EXTRA-FORT, 1940s, yellow gold, mechanical movement with chronograph

EBERHARD & CO. 8 JOURS,
late 1990s, stainless steel,
mechanical movement with
power-reserve indicator

EBERHARD & CO. CHRONO 4,
2000s, stainless steel, self-
winding mechanical movement
with chronograph and date

Elgin

Elgin, along with brands such as Bulova, Illinois, Waltham, Gruen, and Hamilton, was one of the great American watch manufacturers. Founded in Elgin, Illinois, in the penultimate year of the Civil War, the company soon produced more watches than any other in the United States. Elgin also founded a watchmakers' college and built an observatory to broadcast astronomical time signals.

By the 1920s about half of Elgin's manufacturing output was wristwatches (the other half was pocket watches); for many years this made it the country's leading source of wristwatches (companies such as Hamilton were producing far more pocket watches). In particular, the company's Lord Elgin line of higher-end models was a strong commercial success.

During World War II, Elgin made military equipment such as shell fuses and military clocks; after the war it tried to return to serving its prewar market but foundered. Timex (the former Waterbury Watch Company) took over the low end of the marketplace, and Elgin couldn't come up with a competitive strategy. It tried various ideas, such as marketing an electric watch, but was not as successful as Bulova with its Accutron model. Soon Elgin began closing its plants, and in the 1960s, was forced out of business. Since then the name Elgin has been bought and sold, and today it is attached to a series of watches with Japanese quartz movements.

Overall, in its heyday, Elgin produced about sixty million watches, meaning that there are plenty of old models available to collectors. These are far more popular in the United States than in Europe or Asia, and at any moment thousands of old Elgins are available online at eBay and other Websites. Some of them can go for high prices, especially the 1930s-era doctor's duo-dials and the 1950s-era anniversary watches, which are cased in 18-karat gold, but it is also possible to purchase for surprisingly little a humble Elgin mechanical watch that has run for almost a century and, with normal maintainance, will run for another one.

CLOCKWISE FROM TOP LEFT:
LORD ELGIN, 1930s, white gold, mechanical movement

LORD ELGIN, 1940s, white gold filled, mechanical movement

LORD ELGIN, 1940s, yellow gold filled, mechanical movement

LORD ELGIN, 1930s, yellow gold, mechanical movement

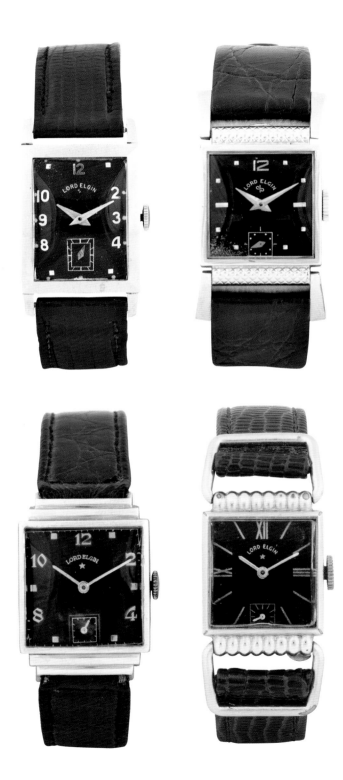

ELGIN DELUXE, 1938,
yellow gold filled, mechanical
movement

ABOVE: **LORD ELGIN CHEVRON**,
1950s, yellow gold filled,
mechanical movement

RIGHT: **ELGIN**, 1920s, yellow
gold filled, mechanical
movement

Eterna

Eterna has been making high-quality watches for 150 years. For a small company, it has achieved a number of successes, including producing novelties such as the first alarm wristwatch (in 1914), the first cigarette-lighter watch (in 1926), and an eight-day alarm watch (in the early 1930s).

Perhaps the company's biggest year was 1948, when it developed the ball-bearing-mounted rotor for self-winding movements. The five balls involved soon became the company's trademark symbol, and today all Eterna watches feature a dial with five small circles under the twelve-hour marker.

However, the brand's primary contribution to the watch world was its movement company, spun off from Eterna in the 1930s and eventually developed into the company known as ETA, the largest and best-known of all the Swiss movement manufacturers.

Eterna is now solely owned by Porsche Design (which had formerly contracted with IWC to produce its watches). It has moderately priced and nicely designed models; among Eterna's best watches are its retro-look series of 1935 Automatics, but its most famous model is the Eternamatic Kon-Tiki. This sports watch was used by Norwegian explorer and anthropologist Thor Heyerdahl and his crew when they crossed the Pacific Ocean in a small wooden raft to prove that Peruvians could have sailed to Polynesia many centuries earlier. Heyerdahl's crew, raft, and the watches all made it safely forty-three hundred miles across the Pacific in ninety-seven days.

RIGHT: **ETERNA SONIC KONTIKI**, 1970s, stainless steel, electronic movement with day and date

FAR RIGHT: **ETERNA KONTIKI FOUR HANDS**, 2000s, stainless steel, self-winding mechanical movement with date

ETERNA, 1990s, stainless steel, self-winding mechanical movement with chronograph and date

ETERNA, 1950s, stainless steel, mechanical movement with chronograph

ETERNA KONTIKI DIVER,
2000s, stainless steel, self-winding mechanical movement with date and power-reserve indicator; water-resistant to 1,000 meters

F. P. Journe

F. P. Journe is only seven years old; its eponymous master, François-Paul Journe (b. 1957), not yet fifty, is already considered one of the geniuses of the watch world, having constructed a pocket watch with a tourbillon when he was only twenty years old.

The company produces only about six hundred watches a year, yet has become instantly successful with its unusual off-center dials and its array of interesting complications, including independent, resonating balance wheels and a tourbillon with *remontoire*, both never before seen in a wristwatch. An F. P. Journe watch looks like no other, although the designs are increasingly being imitated.

Among watchmakers the company has an excellent standing, due in part to Journe's dazzling reputation. And its watches, all of which display the company's motto, *Invenit et Fecit* (Latin for "invented and manufactured"), are already showing up at auction, holding their own against others from makers with histories twenty times longer.

F. P. JOURNE OCTA RÉSERVE DE MARCHE, 2001, platinum, self-winding mechanical movement with date and power-reserve indicator

Francois-Paul Journe makes forward-thinking yet historically informed choices in his creative complications, many of which are unique in the watch world. The Chronométre à Résonance has two complete movements whose balances beat in sympathy to each other, improving the overall timekeeping. The Tourbillon Souverain has a remontoir, a complicated device that regulates the power flow to the escapement.

F. P. JOURNE TOURBILLON SOUVERAIN REMONTOIR D'EGALITÉ AVEC SECONDE MORTE, 2005, platinum, mechanical movement with tourbillon and power-reserve indicator

F. P. JOURNE TOURBILLON SOUVERAIN REMONTOIR D'EGALITÉ, 2001, platinum, mechanical movement with tourbillon and power-reserve indicator

F. P. JOURNE CHRONOMÈTRE À RÉSONANCE, 2001, platinum, two mechanical movements with power-reserve indicator

F. P. JOURNE OCTA
CHRONOGRAPH, 2002,
platinum, self-winding
mechanical movement with
chronograph and date

F. P. JOURNE OCTA
CALENDAR, 2002, platinum,
self-winding mechanical
movement with triple-date
calendar

Franck Muller

One of the most successful of the new eponymous brands, Franck Muller's watches are unusually designed, extra large, and complicated.

Muller (b. 1958), from Switzerland, has always been fond of complications, and his line includes tourbillons, minute repeaters, equations of time, leap-year indicators, split-seconds chronographs, and others.

In 1983, he created the first watch bearing the name Franck Muller (a rectangular model with a day-date calendar and moon-phase indicator), but the company Franck Muller wasn't established until 1992, the same year the first Franck Muller store opened.

In 1992, working with a preexisting sonnerie movement by L. E. Piguet, Muller created a watch containing a grande and petite sonnerie and minute repeater for the hours, quarters, and minutes; a perpetual calendar programmed to the year 2100 with monthly retrograde equation; a leap-year cycle; a twenty-four-hour moon-phase indicator; and an indicator of the internal temperature of the mechanism. This achievement, along with other technological breakthroughs, lend credence to his self-proclaimed moniker, the Master of Complications.

Two of the company's most successful models are the Long Island and the Cintrée Curvex, both of which are available in many variations and with numerous complications. The company issues limited editions of all its models, which is one reason these watches often hold their value better in resale than many competitors.

The Franck Muller company also runs Switzerland's Watchland, a kind of mini-Disneyland for watch lovers.

FRANCK MULLER CINTRÉE CURVEX CASA-BLANCA, c. 2000, stainless steel, self-winding mechanical movement

FRANCK MULLER MASTER BANKER HAVANA, c. 2000, yellow gold, self-winding mechanical movement with date and three time zones

FRANCK MULLER LONG ISLAND CRAZY HOURS, 1990s, white gold, self-winding mechanical movement

LEFT: **FRANCK MULLER CHRONOGRAPHE À DOUBLE FACE,** c. 2000, pink gold, self-winding mechanical movement with chronograph (front and back)

**FRANCK MULLER TRANS-
AMERICA BIG BEN**, 2001,
stainless steel, self-winding
mechanical movement
with date, two time zones,
and alarm

**FRANCK MULLER PLATINUM
DOUBLE-FACE NO. 3,** 1990s,
platinum, self-winding
mechanical movement with
perpetual calendar, equation of
time, moon-phase indicator,
and chronograph on the
reverse face

RIGHT: **FRANCK MULLER**, 1990s, yellow gold, self-winding mechanical movement with split-seconds chronograph

FAR RIGHT: **FRANCK MULLER CINTRÉE CURVEX QUANTIÈME PERPÉTUEL BIRETRO**, C. 2000, yellow gold, self-winding mechanical movement with chronograph, perpetual calendar, and moon-phase indicator

BELOW: **FRANCK MULLER CINTRÉE CURVEX MAGNUM CHRONOGRAPH MASTER CALENDAR**, C. 2000, stainless steel, self-winding mechanical movement with chronograph and triple-date calendar

Franck Muller's cintrée curvex is a deceptively simple looking but difficult-to-execute case with sensuous curves on multiple planes. Unlike many watchmakers who are associated with one or two achievements, Muller is known for a multitude, including his trademark exploding numerals, an extensive range of interesting complications, and unusual retrograde displays.

Gérald Genta

Gérald Genta (b. 1931), is one of the industry's most outstanding designers, responsible for a remarkable series of successes, including Audemars Piguet's Royal Oak, Patek Philippe's Nautilus, Omega's Titane and Constellation, IWC's Da Vinci and Ingenieur, Cartier's Pasha, and the Bulgari-Bulgari for, yes, Bulgari.

Genta, a native of Switzerland, eventually founded his own company in the early 1990s, and went on to design some of the more outrageous and interesting watches of the decade. With tourbillons and retro hours, as well as Mickey Mouse and Donald Duck dials, the company approaches design with a lighter heart and a surer hand than most of its competitors.

Gérald Genta, the company, along with Daniel Roth's brand, is now a part of the Bulgari group, and Gérald Genta, the person, is no longer with the company; today he is launching a new brand.

Few of Gérald Genta's watches are simple — even the entry-level watches tend to have interesting features such as retrograde seconds or jump hours — but some of them are among the most complicated ever made. The Grande Sonnerie features an eight-layered case that has a minute repeater combined with a Westminster chime, and a grand strike. In total, the watch has more than one thousand parts.

LEFT: **GÉRALD GENTA**, 1990s, platinum, self-winding mechanical movement with perpetual calendar and moon-phase indicator

RIGHT: **GÉRALD GENTA**, 1990s, yellow gold and hardwood, self-winding mechanical movement with perpetual calendar and moon-phase indicator

ABOVE AND RIGHT: **GÉRALD GENTA NO. 2**, 1990s, yellow gold, self-winding mechanical movement with tourbillon, perpetual calendar, and moon-phase indicator

Although Gérald Genta no longer works for his eponymous company, which is now owned by Bulgari, his concepts still inform its watches. These include playful, retro-grade displays; the use of some of the cartoon world's favorite images; and extremely demand-ing complications.

ABOVE LEFT: **GÉRALD GENTA MICKEY MOUSE NO. 1**, 1990s, yellow and white gold, self-winding mechanical movement with minute repeater

GÉRALD GENTA FANTASY RACING (unique piece), 2005, white gold, self-winding mechanical movement

RIGHT: **GÉRALD GENTA RETRO DISNEY**, 1990s, white gold, self-winding mechanical movement

GÉRALD GENTA RÉTRO CLASSIC, 1990s, pink gold, mechanical movement

GÉRALD GENTA BIRETRO, 2000, stainless steel, self-winding mechanical movement with date

GÉRALD GENTA SUCCESS AUTOMATIC, 1990s, white gold, self-winding mechanical movement with perpetual calendar and moon-phase indicator

GÉRALD GENTA CHRONO SPORT, c. 2004, stainless steel, self-winding mechanical movement with chronograph and date

Girard-Perregaux

Although the company is more than two hundred years old, Girard-Perregaux is named for the man who bought it in 1852, Constant Girard (1825–1903). (Shortly thereafter Girard married the daughter of a local watchmaker, and added his wife's surname, Perregaux, to the name of the company.)

Girard-Perregaux has won many awards for its design and movements, but one of its greatest contributions to the history of the wristwatch occurred in 1879, when the German Navy commissioned watches attached to leather straps so they could be tied on the wrist — possibly the first mass production of watches specifically for men's wrists.

In the mid-nineteenth century Girard-Perregaux devoted itself to chronometry and especially tourbillons, and in 1884 it created one of the great iconic designs, the tourbillon under Three Gold Bridges. It was so successful as a timekeeper at observatory competitions — not to mention so artistically rendered — that at a 1901 exhibition in Paris it was ruled ineligible to compete on the grounds that it could not be equaled.

In the mid-twentieth century Girard-Perregaux worked on improving automatic wristwatch chronometers; in 1957 it launched its Gyromatic line, fitted with a revolutionary reversing system. In 1967 it earned fully 70 percent of the chronometer certificates awarded by Neuchâtel and became one of a handful of brands ever to sell observatory-tested chronometers to the public.

Unlike most Swiss brands, Girard-Perregaux jumped into the quartz-watch field, pioneering the use of the universally accepted standard frequency for quartz crystal regulators: 32,768 hertz. Although it produced high-grade, high-accuracy quartz movements in-house, ultimately, like most companies, Girard-Perregaux could not compete with the less-expensive Japanese quartz watches.

By the early 1990s the company was down on its luck and was sold to Italian entrepreneur Luigi Macaluso, who gambled on the mechanical comeback and won. Girard-Perregaux is now a high-end manufacturer, part of Macaluso's SoWind Group, which also owns the JeanRichard brands, the SoWind movement manufacturer, and EMG, a case, bracelet, and watch-component manufacturer.

Over the years, Girard-Perregaux has produced ebauches (raw or unfinished movements) for many leading watch companies, including Cartier, Vacheron Constantin, and Ebel, a venerable Swiss company with an interesting history and watches designed in a distinctive shape. Today Girard-Perregaux is one of the few large, independent Swiss watch companies, manufacturing about twenty thousand watches a year, mostly with its own movements, cases, bracelets, and watch parts.

FAR LEFT: **GIRARD-PERREGAUX WORLD TIME CHRONOGRAPH**, c. 2000, pink gold, self-winding mechanical movement with chronograph, date, and world time

BELOW: **GIRARD-PERREGAUX POUR FERRARI**, 2000s, stainless steel, self-winding mechanical movement

GIRARD-PERREGAUX OPERA ONE CARILLON WESTMINSTER (unique piece), 2000, platinum, mechanical movement with tourbillon and minute repeater on Westminster chimes

RIGHT: **GIRARD-PERREGAUX TOURBILLON SOUS TROIS PONTS D'OR AUTOMATIQUE,** 1990s, platinum, self-winding mechanical movement with tourbillon

RIGHT: **GIRARD-PERREGAUX TOURBILLON SOUS TROIS PONTS D'OR AUTOMATIQUE,** 1999, yellow gold, self-winding mechanical movement with tourbillon

GIRARD-PERREGAUX VINTAGE CHRONOGRAPH, 2001, white gold, self-winding mechanical movement with chronograph

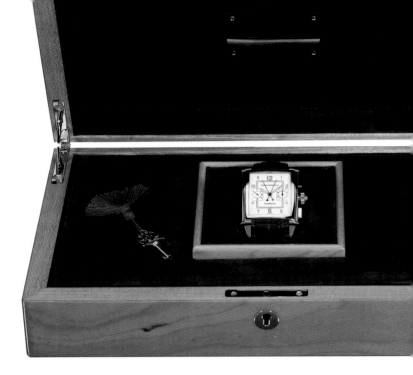

RIGHT: **GIRARD-PERREGAUX VINTAGE 1945 LARGE DATE MOON PHASE** movement

RIGHT BELOW: **GIRARD-PERREGAUX VINTAGE 1945 LARGE DATE MOON PHASE,** 2001, gold, self-winding mechanical movement with date and moon-phase indicator

LEFT: **GIRARD-PERREGAUX VINTAGE CHRONOGRAPH À RATTRAPANTE FOUDROY-ANTE,** c. 2000, pink gold, self-winding mechanical movement with split-seconds chronograph and foudroyante

GIRARD-PERREGAUX POUR FERRARI CHRONOGRAPH F2004, 2004, titanium, self-winding mechanical movement with chronograph, date, and day/night indicator

GIRARD-PERREGAUX POUR FERRARI CHRONOGRAPH NO. 25, late 1990s, yellow gold, self-winding mechanical movement with split-seconds chronograph

GIRARD-PERREGAUX SEA HAWK II, 2000s, stainless steel, self-winding mechanical movement with date and power-reserve indicator; water resistant to 300 meters

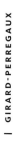

Glashütte Original

Glashütte Original can claim a 150-year-old legacy, but its current success as a prestigious watch brand stems from its renaissance in the 1990s.

Glashütte is a village in Saxony where watchmaking giant Adolf Lange was born (see A. Lange & Söhne). For many years the company Lange established was Germany's most important and successful, but when Saxony ended up behind the Iron Curtain, several German watch companies, including Glashütte, were consolidated into one large watchmaker that produced standard-grade watches for a low-end market.

After the fall of the Iron Curtain, the company, then known as GUB (Glashütte Uhrenbetrieben GmbH), tried to raise its fortunes and started manufacturing high-end timepieces. From these beginnings rose the new Glashütte Original, a German watch with its own in-house movements and well-designed dials and cases.

Success came quickly, and the company's line of heavy, large, and complicated watches flourished. In 2000, the Swatch Group bought the brand but allowed it to retain its German style.

A look at the company's product line reveals a similarity to present-day Lange models; both brands also compete for the title of rightful heir to the great watchmaker Adolf Lange (Glashütte Original possesses most of Adolf Lange's archives; Lange retails the name). For the most part, Glashütte Original watches are less expensive than those of Lange; they also do well at holding their resale value.

Among the brand's most successful watches are the models in the PanoDate line, especially the PanoGraph and the PanoRetroGraph, which has won numerous awards. Glashütte Original also produces a line of marine chronometers and several special edition timepieces, including one dedicated to Julius Assman, a native of the town of Glashütte and one of the great watchmakers of the nineteenth century. Glashütte Original recently relocated to a new building that also houses the Glashütte watch museum.

Union, Glashütte Original's sister brand, also manufactures quality watches with movements that the company produces. These watches, priced far lower than Glashütte Original's, are not retailed in the United States, but occasionally show up online and at auction.

GLASHÜTTE ORIGINAL CLASSIC REGULATOR, 1990s, yellow gold, mechanical movement

GLASHÜTTE ORIGINAL PANOMATICTOURBILLON, 2000s, platinum, self-winding mechanical movement with tourbillon and date

**GLASHÜTTE ORIGINAL
KARRÉE AUF UND AB,** 1990s,
stainless steel, mechanical
movement with moon-phase
display and power-reserve
indicator

**GLASHÜTTE ORIGINAL
ALFRED HELWIG TOURBILLON
2,** c. 2000, platinum,
mechanical movement with
date, power-reserve indicator,
and tourbillon

If Breguet can claim
special privilege to using
the tourbillon in its models, Glashütte Original
can do the same for the
flying tourbillon (a tourbillon whose cage is sup-
ported only on one side),
which was invented in
the Glashütte region by
Alfred Helwig.

GLASHÜTTE ORIGINAL PANOGRAPH, 2004, pink gold, mechanical movement with chronograph and date. The thirty-minute register on this chronograph has a unique configuration

The distinguishing features of Glashütte Original's pano-movements are the three-quarter-plate bridge work, typical of Saxon watchmaking, the engraved balance cocks screwed in gold chatons, and the traditional technical refinements.

**GLASHÜTTE ORIGINAL
PANOMATICLUNAR**, 2000s,
platinum, self-winding
mechanical movement with
date and moon-phase indicator

Gruen

The American brand Gruen was founded by German-born watchmaker Dietrich Grün (1847–1911) who for lack of an umlaut in the new world, changed his name to something Americans could more easily spell: Gruen.

The watchmaker set up his organization in Columbus, Ohio, but imported all of his movements from his native Germany and then from Switzerland. Gruen began making wristwatches in 1908; after Dietrich died three years later, his son Frederick became the company's president. Soon Gruen was making solid, dependable watches that helped the company to become the country's largest watchmaker.

After Frederick's death, the family sold the firm. It continued to make more than a half million watches every year.

In the late 1950s, Gruen moved to New York City (and all its records in Ohio were destroyed). Two decades later, Gruen bet heavily on LCD watches, reducing its production of mechanical ones and ignoring quartz. The gamble did not pay off, and although the LCF Telestar model sold well for a short time, the company eventually went bankrupt.

Today, modern watches bearing the Gruen name are on the market, but these timepieces are actually Chinese-made, with Japanese quartz movements. However, large numbers of vintage Gruens are available; like Elgins, some of them, particularly the 18-karat-gold doctor's-dial watches and some of the Curvex models, are in great demand. (These watches often used movements bought from the Swiss company Aegler, which also supplied Rolex, meaning that many vintage Rolex Princes on the market are actually recased Gruens. Be wary.)

GRUEN, 1930s, yellow gold, mechanical movement

GRUEN CURVEX, 1930s, stainless steel, mechanical movement

OPPOSITE, CLOCKWISE FROM TOP LEFT:

GRUEN PAN AMERICAN, 1943, yellow gold filled, mechanical movement

GRUEN PAN AMERICAN ACE, 1940s, yellow gold filled, mechanical movement

GRUEN DAY/NIGHT, 1950s, yellow gold filled, mechanical movement with day/night indicator

GRUEN CHRONO TIMER, 1940s, stainless steel, mechanical movement with chronograph

LEFT TO RIGHT:

GRUEN, 1930s, yellow gold filled, mechanical movement

GRUEN, 1930s, Guildite, mechanical movement

GRUEN, 1940s, white gold filled, mechanical movement

Hamilton

Hamilton was the American Patek Philippe, the best and most authentic of the watchmaking companies in the United States. It made high-grade movements in an American style of finish (less fussy than the Swiss, but functionally uncompromised).

The company, founded in 1892 in Lancaster, Pennsylvania, quickly garnered acclaim selling highly accurate timepieces to the railroad industry. It also produced some excellent marine chronometers during World War I, and it became the official watch of American airmail companies, as well as many airlines.

Throughout the 1920s and 1930s, Hamilton created many beautiful art deco watches, including the Piping Rock and Spur models. And in the 1940s, Hamilton once again supplied the military (this time the army) with watches.

In the 1950s, Hamilton lit up the watch world with its Venturas and Pacers, electric models created by famed designer Richard Arbib. Rather than conventional squares or circles, the watch's irregularly cased watches resembled large triangles, highlighted with futuristic-looking numerals and hands, as though designed for the old television cartoon show *The Jetsons*.

Other electric models followed, such as the Altair (1962) and the Gemini (1963). Then, to stem the coming tide of quartz watches, as well as the highly successful Bulova Accutron, the company devised its Pulsar model, a transistorized watch with an LED display that became very popular; in fact, there was a waiting list to purchase certain models.

But the Hamilton empire began to crumble in the late 1970s, when other more accurate and cheaper watches stole Pulsar's market share. The company fractured into several parts, and eventually the electronic watch division was sold to the Japanese company Seiko.

Meanwhile, another part of Hamilton entered into a business arrangement with the Buren Watch Company in Switzerland; soon many of Hamilton's movements came from Buren, including its popular micro-rotor Thin-O-Matic; other movements were supplied by ETA. The company became progressively European, and was soon bought by the Swiss company SSIH (see Swatch).

Today, the Hamilton brand is a solid entry-level label for the Swatch Group but a far cry from its former glory. (And its former plant in Lancaster, topped by two beautiful clock towers, is now a residential condominium.)

On the collectors' market, a vintage Hamilton in good shape is a watch to look out for, particularly when cased in platinum or white gold, as some of the art deco models were,

or the increasingly rare Ventura and Pacer. These models were recently reissued by Hamilton and are sometimes sold as *Men in Black* watches, as they were featured in the movie of the same name.

Disappointed watch connoisseurs often refer to Hamilton as the "brand that could have been great."

ABOVE TOP: **HAMILTON SQUARE ENAMEL**, 1926-27, white gold with enamel inlay, mechanical movement

ABOVE: **HAMILTON LANGLEY**, 1929-33, white gold, mechanical movement

ABOVE TOP: **HAMILTON OVAL**, 1928, white filled gold with enamel inlay, mechanical movement

ABOVE: **HAMILTON CORONADO**, 1929-32, white gold with enamel inlay, mechanical movement

HAMILTON PIPING ROCK, 1928–32, yellow gold with enamel inlay, mechanical movement

ABOVE RIGHT: **HAMILTON SECKRON,** 1935, yellow gold filled, mechanical movement

HAMILTON MOUNT VERNON, 1932–34, white gold filled, mechanical movement

HAMILTON ANDREWS, 1931–34, white gold, mechanical movement

HAMILTON OAKMONT, 1931–34, white gold, mechanical movement

HAMILTONS, 1953

TOP ROW, LEFT TO RIGHT:
RYAN, LINDSAY, CRAIG, GROVER

MIDDLE ROW, LEFT TO RIGHT:
CRANSTON, BRENT, BELDON, SHERWOOD

BOTTOM ROW, LEFT TO RIGHT:
EMERY, MEDFORD, CARLTON, ALAN

All mechanical movements

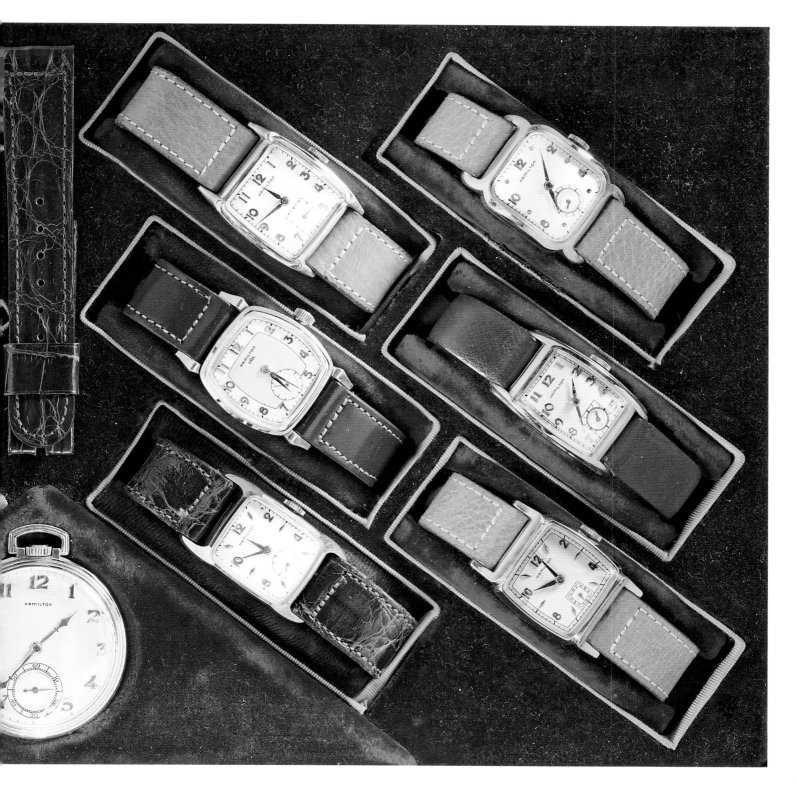

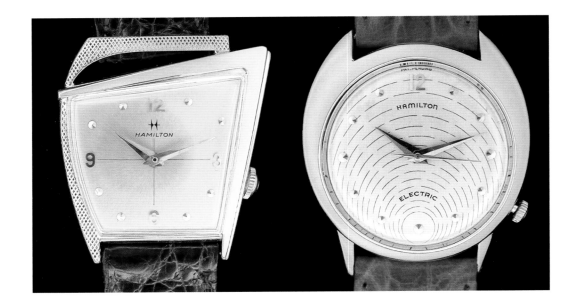

HAMILTON PEGASUS, 1960s, gold filled, electric movement

HAMILTON POLARIS, 1960s, yellow gold, electric movement

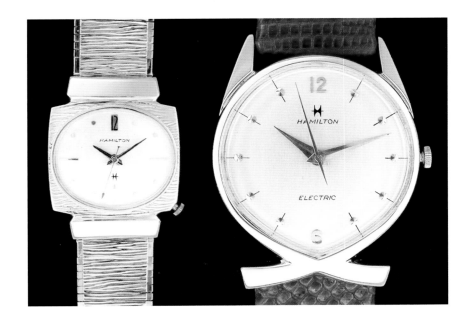

HAMILTON VEGA, c. 1960, yellow gold filled, electric movement

Richard Arbib, who designed the cases and dials of the Hamilton electrics, claimed that the shape of the Ventura was inspired by fins he had designed for World War II bombs and then for 1950s automobiles.

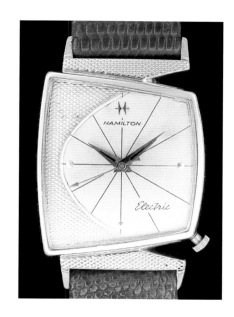

HAMILTON EVEREST, c. 1958, yellow gold filled, electric movement

HAMILTON METEOR, c. 1960, yellow gold filled, electric movement

HAMILTON VENTURA, c. 1957, yellow gold, electric movement

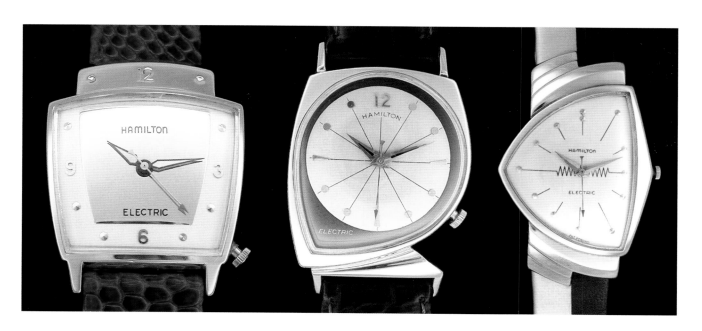

Harry Winston

Founded by Los Angeleno Harry Winston (1896–1978), Harry Winston jewelers has been making watches for more than two decades. These pieces tend to be large, fancy, and expensive. The company's design trademark is a set of huge triple-arched lugs.

In 2001, Harry Winston launched Rare Timepieces under Max Busser, which teamed with some of the best independent watchmakers in the business, including F. P. Journe, Vianney Halter, Peter Speake-Marin, Felix Baumgartner, and Christophe Claret, to create some truly groundbreaking watches. Known as the Opus series, these timepieces are often beautifully jeweled yet retain an emphasis on technical watchmaking.

HARRY WINSTON PROJECT Z1, 2004, zalium, self-winding mechanical movement with chronograph

TOP RIGHT: **HARRY WINSTON OPUS 4** back: date and moon-phase indicator

RIGHT: **HARRY WINSTON OPUS 4** (developed with Christophe Claret), 2004, platinum, mechanical movement with tourbillon, time indicators on both sides. Front: minute repeater on cathedral gongs

**HARRY WINSTON PROJECT
Z2 DIVER**, 2004, zalium with
platinum bezel, self-winding
mechanical movement with
chronograph and date; water-
resistant to 200 meters

RIGHT: **HARRY WINSTON OPUS 3** prototype developed with Vianney Halter, 2003 (production models not yet released), rose gold, mechanical movement with date

FAR RIGHT: **HARRY WINSTON OPUS 3** prototype movement

BOTTOM LEFT: **HARRY WINSTON OPUS 1 RESON-2** developed with F. P. Journe, 2001, platinum, two mechanical movements with power-reserve indicator

BOTTOM RIGHT: **HARRY WINSTON OPUS 1 TOURB-1** developed with F. P. Journe, 2001, platinum with diamonds, mechanical movement with tourbillon and power-reserve indicator

HARRY WINSTON OPUS V
developed with Felix
Baumgartner, 2005, pink gold,
mechanical movement with
power-reserve and day/night
indicators

Hublot

The Swiss firm Hublot, founded in 1980, had a single-minded approach to watch design: "Hublot" is French for porthole, which is, more or less, what all the company's watches resemble. Few manufacturers (Daniel Roth and Ebel come to mind) have been as focussed in marketing watches of one shape. Hublot's watches were designed to be simple and clean, with no unnecessary elements; twelve titanium screws secured the bezel to the case so that the screws, rather than digits, could be used to mark the hours. They were placed on high-quality vanilla-scented rubber straps, which were mocked at first but have since been emulated by many others.

Hublot's watches are popular in Europe — particularly in Spain. Still an independent company, Hublot is now run by Jean-Claude Biver, the man who revived Blancpain. Biver's ambition, as well as his panache, can be seen in the recently introduced, aggressively styled — and aggressively marketed — Big Bang chronograph.

HUBLOT REGULATEUR, 2000s, pink gold, self-winding mechanical movement with date

HUBLOT CLASSIC, 2000s, stainless steel, self-winding mechanical movement with date

LEFT: **HUBLOT TWO TIME ZONES,** 1990s, yellow gold, self-winding mechanical movement with date and two time zones

HUBLOT BIG BANG, 2005, red gold, self-winding mechanical movement with chronograph and date

IWC

The International Watch Company (IWC) is the only major Swiss watch company founded by an American. In 1868, twenty-seven-year-old Massachusetts resident Florentine Ariosto Jones decided to build a watch factory in Switzerland so he could supply the United States with well-made but inexpensive movements. Jones joined up with watchmaker Johann Heinrich Moser, whose hometown of Schaffhausen was located in the German-speaking part of Switzerland; here a hydroelectric plant had recently been built, generating low-cost energy.

Despite the company's intelligent business strategy and well-manufactured watches, the grand plan crashed. Running into high tariffs and other difficulties when trying to enter the American market, Jones found limited success there. When his machinery began to fail, the company did too. By 1875, it was bankrupt. Another American, Frederick Seeland, took over, and IWC fared somewhat better — but only for a short time. A third owner then acquired it: Johann Rauschenbach-Vogel, an IWC executive whose family subsequently held on to IWC for four generations.

The company prospered through the early part of the twentieth century, and although the Depression caused another downturn, IWC stayed afloat, in part because it always strove for innovation; as early as 1899, the company had started using its own small, 64-caliber women's pocket-watch movement for a series of men's wristwatches. During World War I, it began manufacturing its own 75-caliber men's wristwatch movement.

One of the company's best decisions came when it strove to meet the demands of its Portuguese agents, who were requesting an oversized watch. In response, the company produced the Portuguese, a large wristwatch with a

pocket-watch movement. The model, resurrected by the company in 1993, remains one of its most successful.

In the late 1930s came the Mark IX, an anti-magnetic watch designed specifically for pilots. The series has continued; today's model is the Mark XV. An early Mark in good condition is among the most prized items at watch auctions, as is the Mark XI, with its famous 89-caliber movement.

During the war, the Allies bombed the IWC factory in Schaffhausen. The plant survived and continued making timepieces. In fact, after the war, despite losing its Eastern European market due to the Soviet occupation, IWC prospered by reestablishing its old connections in other countries, especially the United States. And it successfully introduced new models, such as the Ingenieur, which Sir Edmund Hillary wore on his trek to the peak of Mount Everest.

In the late 1970s the company was once again in financial trouble but was rescued by VDO, a German industrial conglomerate. It then began a long-term (but now defunct) cooperation with designer F. A. Porsche of the automobile dynasty.

In 1991, IWC director Günther Blümlein founded LMH; the company owned all of IWC as well as 90 percent of A. Lange & Söhne and 60 percent of Jaeger-LeCoultre (Audemars Piguet owned the other 40 percent). As mentioned previously, Richemont bought LMH in 2000.

Although the company has relied heavily on internally modified, outsourced movements during the last few decades, it has recently begun to focus more attention on developing and manufacturing movements in-house.

Throughout its history, IWC fans have enjoyed the brand's engineering-oriented mentality and straightforward design; it is one of the few companies that still performs assembly, oiling, timing, and finishing by hand.

ABOVE LEFT: **IWC INGENIEUR SL**, late 1970s, stainless steel, self-winding mechanical movement with date; this model was designed by Gérald Genta

ABOVE RIGHT: **IWC INGENIEUR**, mid-1960s, stainless steel, self-winding mechanical movement with date

LEFT: **IWC INGENIEUR CHRONOGRAPH AMG**, 2005, titanium, self-winding mechanical movement with chronograph

ABOVE: **IWC PORTOFINO**, 1980s, yellow gold, mechanical movement with moon-phase indicator

IWC NOVECENTO AUTOMATIC PERPETUAL, c. 2000, yellow gold, self-winding mechanical movement with perpetual calendar and moon-phase indicator

FAR LEFT: **IWC DA VINCI JUBILEE RATTRAPANTE**, 1995, platinum, self-winding mechanical movement with split-seconds chronograph, perpetual calendar, and moon-phase indicator

LEFT: **IWC PORTOFINO PERPETUEL**, 1990s, platinum, mechanical movement with perpetual calendar and moon-phase indicator

IWC is a technical engineering brand that has built its longterm success on a few easily identifiable lines, such as the Portuguese, the Da Vinci, the Portofino, the recently revitalized Ingenieur, and the company's famous pilot's watches.

Although many highly complicated watches can be finicky, IWC has a reputation for designing and manufacturing complications that work by using well-tested, tried-and-true movements as a base.

IWC PORTUGUESE MINUTE REPEATER, 2000s, white gold, mechanical movement with minute repeater

ABOVE: **IWC PORTUGUESE PERPETUAL CALENDAR**, 2005, rose gold, self-winding mechanical movement with perpetual calendar, and moon-phase and power-reserve indicators

RIGHT: **IWC GRANDE COMPLICATION**, 2004, yellow gold, self-winding mechanical movement with chronograph, perpetual calendar, minute repeater, and moon-phase indicator

IWC SPITFIRE DOPPELCHRONOGRAPH, 2000s, stainless steel, self-winding mechanical movement with split-seconds chronograph and day and date

BELOW TOP: **IWC AQUATIMER**, 2000s, stainless steel, self-winding mechanical movement with date; water-resistant to 1,000 meters

BELOW BOTTOM: **IWC AQUATIMER** luminous dial

The Mark XI was IWC's first megastar wristwatch, originally produced under a British Ministry of Defense contract as a specially designed pilot's watch. Specifications called for a "highly accurate timepiece, suitable for astro-navigational purposes." The watch was produced from 1948 until at least 1979, and probably the early 1980s.

IWC MARK XI, c. 1948, stainless steel, mechanical movement

ABOVE: **IWC PORTUGUESE CHRONOGRAPH RATTRA-PANTE**, 1990s, platinum, mechanical movement with split-seconds chronograph

For its Portuguese line, IWC made a bold commitment to the large-watch trend by creating a technologically sophisticated movement that required a forty-two millimeter case. The watch has a seven-day power reserve. Its mainspring is long enough to last for eight and a half days, but there is a stop mechanism that halts the movement after seven to prevent it from running in an inaccurate state.

RIGHT: **IWC PORTUGUESE AUTOMATIC**, 2000s, stainless steel, self-winding mechanical movement with date and power-reserve indicator

RIGHT: **IWC PORTUGUESE AUTOMATIC** movement

Jaeger-LeCoultre

Mention the name Jaeger-LeCoultre (or, more familiarly, JLC) to people who like watches and they usually think of its trademark model, the Reverso. Mention the name to connoisseurs, and they will tell you that few companies can match Jaeger-LeCoultre's long history of well-manufactured watches. Not only has the company produced high-quality timepieces throughout its nearly 175-year history, but it has also made movements for such brands as Vacheron Constantin, Audemars Piguet, IWC, Breguet, and Patek Philippe.

The LeCoultre part of Jaeger-LeCoultre dates back to 1833, when Antoine LeCoultre (1883-1881) opened a watch factory in Le Sentier, Switzerland (not far from where the current factory stands). LeCoultre was a gifted watchmaker: In 1844, he invented the millionometer, the first instrument capable of measuring components to the nearest micron, or millionth of a meter; in 1847, he developed a crown winding system that set the time.

LeCoultre established a reputation for innovation and quality, and his company flourished, becoming the leading supplier of movements, parts, and tools to the Swiss watchmaking industry. LeCoultre's company also produced complicated movements, repeaters, chronographs, calendars, and innovations such as the world's flattest pocket-watch caliber, a 1.38-millimeter-high movement (in 1903).

In 1925, David LeCoultre, grandson of the firm's founder, merged his company with that of Edmond Jaeger (1850-1922), who supplied watch movements to Cartier; the company began selling watches under the name Jaeger-LeCoultre.

The company continued to innovate. In 1928, Jaeger-LeCoultre introduced the Atmos clock, which never needs winding; its power source is the change in air temperature. In 1929 came the world's smallest mechanical movement — the Calibre 101 — weighing less than a gram. And, in 1931, came the Reverso; according to legend, it was designed to help India-based British officers protect their watches while playing polo.

(The Reverso was popular for some time but fell out of vogue until the 1960s, when an Italian dealer, visiting Jaeger-LeCoultre's factory, spotted unused cases sitting in a drawer. He bought them and fitted them with movements; they sold out instantly. Today Reverso models account for a significant portion of the company's total sales.)

In 1932, LeCoultre attempted to buy a majority interest in Patek Philippe, but lost out to Charles and Jean Stern, whose company was already the supplier of the dials used in Patek Philippe watches.

Throughout the rest of the twentieth century, Jaeger-LeCoultre turned out excellent (and highly collectible) mid-priced watches, including the Memovox, one of the most successful alarm watches ever introduced, and the Futurematic, with its small power-reserve indicator. But like IWC, the company ran into tough times during the 1970s; also like IWC, it was rescued by the German company VDO, and today it is owned by Richemont.

Jaeger-LeCoultre is one of the few companies in Switzerland still producing its own movements, cases, dials, hands, and bracelets. Its enduring reputation for being the watchmakers' watchmaker is well deserved.

On the downside, the company has little to offer to sports-watch lovers. The brand is making a concerted effort to rectify this situation with its Compressor line. For the most part, however, if you don't like a simple rectangular or round case, you won't like Jaeger-LeCoultre. Still, it has often been said that there's a little Jaeger-LeCoultre in almost every other brand.

ABOVE LEFT TO RIGHT:
JAEGER-LECOULTRE MEMOVOX, 1950s, yellow gold, mechanical movement with alarm

JAEGER-LECOULTRE MEMOVOX AUTOMATIC, 1970s, stainless steel, self-winding mechanical movement with date and alarm

JAEGER-LECOULTRE MASTER COMPRESSOR MEMOVOX AUTOMATIQUE, 2000s, rose gold, self-winding mechanical movement with date and alarm

FAR LEFT: **JAEGER-LECOULTRE REVERSO**, 1940s, stainless steel and yellow gold, mechanical movement

LEFT: **JAEGER-LECOULTRE MOONPHASE**, 1990s, stainless steel, quartz movement with date and moon-phase indicator

Designer Magali Metrailer, the creator of the modern JLC sports-watch look, is responsible for the Master Compressor design. JLC, which has never had an identifiable sports-watch line, has committed considerable resources to its bold new designs.

JAEGER-LECOULTRE MASTER COMPRESSOR EXTREME WORLD CHRONOGRAPH, 2000s, titanium and stainless steel, self-winding mechanical movement with chronograph, date, power-reserve indicator, and world-time display

OPPOSITE TOP LEFT:
JAEGER-LECOULTRE MASTER COMPRESSOR GEOGRAPHIC, 2000s, stainless steel, self-winding mechanical movement with two time zones and day/night indicator

OPPOSITE TOP RIGHT:
JAEGER-LECOULTRE AMVOX 1 R-ALARM, 2000s, titanium, self-winding mechanical movement with date and alarm

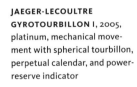

JAEGER-LECOULTRE GYROTOURBILLON I, 2005, platinum, mechanical movement with spherical tourbillon, perpetual calendar, and power-reserve indicator

The new Gyrotourbillon 1, with a multi-axis tour-billon cage milled out of a solid billet of alumi-num and a fifteen-day power reserve, is a tour de force of engineering prowess.

OPPOSITE BOTTOM LEFT:
JAEGER-LECOULTRE MASTER HOMETIME, 2000s, stainless steel, self-winding mechanical movement with date, two time zones, and day/night indicator

OPPOSITE BOTTOM RIGHT:
JAEGER-LECOULTRE MASTER RÉSERVE DE MARCHE, 1998, stainless steel, self-winding mechanical movement with date and power-reserve indicator

OPPOSITE: **JAEGER-LECOULTRE REVERSO CHRONOGRAPHE** (front and back), 1996, pink gold, mechanical movement with chronograph, date, and start/stop indicator

JAEGER-LECOULTRE REVERSO SHADOW, late 1990s, stainless steel and bronze, mechanical movement

JAEGER-LECOULTRE REVERSO GÉOGRAPHIQUE, 1998, pink gold, mechanical movement with multiple time zones and day/night indicator

The Reverso, a watch whose case flips over to reveal a protective back or another face, is a design landmark in horology. The year 2006 is the 75th anniversary of the very first model, and while the Reverso has not been in continuous production all this time, it has become an icon since its reintroduction in the early 1980s. JLC now makes the watches with a vast array of complications, metals, designs, and dials.

JAEGER-LECOULTRE REVERSO QUANTIÈME PERPÉTUEL RETROGRADE, 2000, pink gold, mechanical movement with perpetual calendar, and moon-phase and day/night indicators

JAEGER-LECOULTRE REVERSO PLATINUM NUMBER ONE, 2002, platinum, mechanical movement

Jaquet Droz

This small brand, like many others, is named after a venerated Swiss watchmaker. In this case it is Pierre Jaquet Droz (1721–1790), who was famous for his automatons — robotlike wind-up toys that performed human functions such as signing a name or pouring a cup of tea; others were in the shape of animals, including dogs that barked and birds that sang.

Droz was eventually accused of sorcery, although his unusual machines grew so popular that he never faced serious trouble. Eventually he was invited to present his works to Spain's King Ferdinand VI, who liked them so much that he bought every piece Droz brought with him.

The company disappeared many years ago, but was resurrected in 1995 by two former Breguet employees who bought the rights to the name and assembled and sold replicas of the original Droz automatons. They also began manufacturing mid-grade mechanical watches with modest success.

Since being purchased by the Swatch group in 2003, the company has redefined itself as a small-production, high-grade watch company focusing primarily on small, limited editions. Known for historically inspired designs and exquisitely crafted dials of enamel, precious metals, and exotic stones (often involving exotic decorative techniques), the watches feature unique versions of Frédéric Piguet movements, modified to their specifications, and wrapped in well-designed precious metal cases.

JAQUET DROZ GRANDE SECONDE EMAIL NOIR ARDOISE, 2005, red gold, self-winding mechanical movement

TOP: **JAQUET DROZ GRANDE DATE EMAIL**, 2005, white gold, self-winding mechanical movement with date

ABOVE: **JAQUET DROZ LE DEUX FUSEAUX EMAIL**, 2005, white gold, self-winding mechancal movement with two time zones, date, and twenty-four hour indicator

TOP: **JAQUET DROZ GRANDE SECONDE MEDIUM**, 2005, white gold, self-winding mechanical movement

ABOVE: **JAQUET DROZ QUANTIEME PERPETUEL EMAIL**, 2005, white gold, self-winding mechanical movement with perpetual calendar

TOP: **JAQUET DROZ GRANDE HEURE MINUTE**, 2005, white gold, self-winding mechanical movement

ABOVE: **JAQUET DROZ LES DEUX FUSEAUX REHAUT**, 2005, white gold, self-winding mechancal movement with two time zones, date, and twenty-four hour indicator

TOP: **JAQUET DROZ GRANDE SECONDE CARBONE**, 2005, white gold, self-winding mechanical movement

ABOVE: **JAQUET DROZ QUANTIEME PERPETUEL REHAUT**, 2005, white gold, self-winding mechanical movement with perpetual calendar

JAQUET DROZ GRANDE SECONDE ALGUE PETRIFIÉE (unique piece), 2005, white gold, self-winding mechanical movement. The dial base is made from petrified algae, the world's oldest plant life.

**JAQUET DROZ LES DOUZE
VILLES EMAIL**, 2005, white
gold, self-winding mechanical
movement with world time

JAQUET DROZ LES LUNES EMAIL, 2005, white gold, self-winding mechanical movment with triple-date calendar and moon-phase indicator

Martin Braun

The Martin Braun line is unusual. Some of its offerings are reminiscent of other companies' contemporary watches, but the sunrise and sunset complications on the EOS watch are truly remarkable.

Martin Braun's father was a master goldsmith near the German watchmaking town of Pforzheim, and Braun himself became a master watchmaker at the age of twenty-seven, in 1991. He soon began to work on a watch that could show the time for both sunrise and sunset; almost ten years later in 2000, he unveiled the EOS model and announced his new company.

The Martin Braun watches in the EOS series are immediately recognizable by their extra hands indicating sunrise and sunset. Since the time of sunrise and sunset varies with the geographic position of the observer, the company makes twenty-eight disks that it uses to calibrate watches used in different locales (custom-made discs are available for those who live in parts of the world not covered by the disks).

Martin Braun's newest lines of watches are the Heliozentric, which displays the position of the earth in relation to the sun, and the Astraios, which combines the functions of the Heliozentic and the EOS. The reason he creates such watches? "I am simply fulfilling my own personal fantasy of what I think a watch should do."

Braun has done well in America, where 40 percent of the company's watches are sold; his next biggest market is Hong Kong. He also owns N. B. Yäeger, which produces mechanical pilots' watches and chronographs at prices far lower than his eponymous brand.

TOP LEFT: **MARTIN BRAUN ASTRAIOS**, 2000s, stainless steel, self-winding mechanical movement with date, sunrise/sunset indicator, and display of the earth in relation to the sun

BOTTOM LEFT: **MARTIN BRAUN EOS SQUARE W**, 2000s, stainless steel, mechanical movement with date and sunrise/sunset indicator

TOP RIGHT: **MARTIN BRAUN CHRONO BLUE**, 2000s, stainless steel, mechanical movement with chronograph

BOTTOM RIGHT: **MARTIN BRAUN NOTOS**, 2006, platinum, self-winding mechanical movement with month and date, declination, and equation of time. Declination is the latitude of the sun at noon

MARTIN BRAUN EOS, 2000s, rose gold, self-winding mechanical movement with date and sunrise/sunset indicator

Movado

This company was founded in 1881 by Achilles Ditesheim, but the name Movado didn't appear until 1905. Movado means "always in motion" in Esperanto, the language that was invented by late nineteenth-century idealists to replace all other languages but didn't catch on (today it has fewer than one hundred thousand speakers). As a result, "Movado" is probably Esperanto's best-known word.

The company produced many excellent watches throughout the last century, especially a series of triple-date watches marketed by Tiffany as well as Movado itself. The firm's Polyplan watch (1912) was the first designed to follow the wrist's curve; its 1926 Ermeto was a travel clock whose movement was activated by opening and shutting its case. Furthermore, Movado's chronograph movements were highly regarded by watchmakers and collectors alike.

Movado's most famous model is the Museum watch, designed by Nathan George Horwitt in 1947. The straightforward blank face features a simple dot at the twelve o'clock position, along with an hour and a minute hand. The name refers to the fact that the watch was acquired by New York's Museum of Modern Art for its design collection. The watch is still being issued; today's models come in an array of colors and metals.

Like so many others, the company foundered at midcentury and was bought, first by the American Zenith Radio Corporation and then the North American Watch Company. Today, the Movado Group is a conglomerate based in New Jersey; its brands include Ebel and Concord (once one of the largest Swiss importers to the United States, and best known for its ultra-flat quartz Delirium watches, which used the thinnest movement ever made). Movado also owns the fashion brands Tommy Hilfiger and ESQ, as well as Coach.

LEFT ABOVE: **MOVADO MUSEUM**, 1960s, yellow gold, mechanical movement with date

LEFT BELOW: **MOVADO MUSEUM**, 1960s, yellow gold, mechanical movement with date

BOTTOM LEFT: **MOVADO ERMETO**, 1950s, yellow gold, mechanical movement with date

BOTTOM RIGHT: **MOVADO CALENDERMETO**, c. 1950, yellow gold, mechanical movement with triple-date calendar and moon-phase indicator

ABOVE: **MOVADO**, C. 1950, yellow gold, mechanical movement with triple-date calendar

ABOVE: **MOVADO UPTODATE**, 1940s, stainless steel, mechanical movement with date

RIGHT: **MOVADO FOR TIFFANY**, 1950s, stainless steel, mechanical movement with chronograph

FAR RIGHT: **MOVADO**, 1940s, yellow gold, mechanical movement with chronograph

Nomos

This brand out of Glashütte, Germany, is known for its unusually simple, clean dials, and the good workmanship inside.

The original Nomos company went under many decades ago, but not for lack of sales; instead, its demise resulted from legal battles with other local firms that were unhappy with the company's policy of advertising its Glashütte roots and workmanship, while at the same time undercutting its competitors' prices.

Nomos was resuscitated in 1992 by the German Roland Schwertner; once again, the other Glashütte companies objected to Nomos using the name Glashütte on its dial, but this time the courts sided with Nomos, and the brand now features both brand and place name on its watches.

Nomos is the Greek word connoting a custom or law, and comes from the verb *neimô*, meaning to distribute or dispense, and Nomos watches are distributed at a comparatively low price. Among its best models are the classically designed round Tangente and the square Tetra, both heavily influenced by Bauhaus tradition.

Although Nomos does not make any women's models, its designs are not particularly gender-specific; one-fourth of all Nomos watches are worn by women.

While relying on base movements supplied by ETA, the company has recently begun to manufacture more components in-house, including a traditional gilt-finished, three-quarter plate with blued screws for some of its hand-wound calibers, and an exclusive automatic module for its Tangomat line.

LEFT: **NOMOS TANGENTE DATE POWER RESERVE** (face and movement), 2000s, stainless steel, mechanical movement with date and power-reserve indicator

LEFT: **NOMOS ORION** (face and back), 2000s, stainless steel, mechanical movement

NOMOS TETRA, 2000s, stainless steel, mechanical movement

NOMOS LUDWIG, 2000s, stainless steel, mechanical movement

NOMOS TANGOMAT, 2006, stainless steel, self-winding mechanical movement

NOMOS TANGENTE, stainless
steel, mechanical movement

Officine Panerai

This Italian brand was founded in 1860 by Giovanni Panerai (1825–1897) as a small workshop for mechanical instruments. Within a decade, it was supplying the Italian navy with instruments ranging from fuses to depth-measuring devices.

The company retailed Rolex and Patek Philippe watches while continuing to make and sell optical and mechanical precision instruments to the Italian defense ministry. As business increased, it renamed itself Officine Panerai.

In 1935, it began making wrist-worn depth gauges and compasses; within a year it had produced the prototype for its well-known Radiomir wristwatch. In 1943, a safety lever and bridge device was fitted to the Radiomir, which pressed the crown tightly against the case and also permitted the watch to be wound under water.

For many years, the watches, which used mostly Rolex and Angelus movements, were available only to the Italian Navy, and the company eventually fell on hard times; only when it was resurrected in 1993 did it begin selling to a non-military market.

In 1997, Officine Panerai was purchased by Vendôme Luxury Group, a wholly owned subsidiary of Richemont. It has become a leader in the production of unusually large men's watches worn by movie stars and athletes. The brand has developed an intense cult, and Panerai watch wearers often greet each other as though they were members of a club. This fashion has spawned an entire industry in branded jackets and hats, almost none of which are actually made by the company.

Also extremely popular are vintage Panerais (which the modern watches resemble) but, due to their scarcity, they generally sell for far more than their contemporary counterparts.

RIGHT, TOP TO BOTTOM:
OFFICINE PANERAI, 1943, stainless steel, mechanical movement

OFFICINE PANERAI RADIOMIR 8 GIORNI BREVETTATO, made in 1956 for the Egyptian Navy, aluminum, mechanical movement

OFFICINE PANERAI MARINA MILITARE, 1953, stainless steel, mechanical movement

OFFICINE PANERAI MARINA MILITARE, made in 1953 for the Italian Navy, stainless steel, mechanical movement, designed for left-handed wearers

BELOW: **OFFICINE PANERAI**
RADIOMIR PAM 21, 1997,
platinum, mechanical
movement

RIGHT: **OFFICINE PANERAI**
LUMINOR LOGO, 1993,
stainless steel, mechanical
movement

OFFICINE PANERAI
RADIOMIR PAM 21 back, with
Rolex movement

OFFICINE PANERAI LUMINOR
1950, 2002, stainless steel,
mechanical movement

OFFICINE PANERAI
LUMINOR, 1950s, stainless
steel, mechanical movement

OFFICINE PANERAI MARE
NOSTRUM, 1995, stainless
steel, mechanical movement
with chronograph

OFFICINE PANERAI
RADIOMIR TOURBILLON,
2001, platinum, mechanical
movement with tourbillon

ABOVE LEFT: **OFFICINE
PANERAI RADIOMIR**, 2002,
stainless steel, self-winding
mechanical movement
with date

ABOVE CENTER: **OFFICINE
PANERAI RADIOMIR GMT,**
2003, stainless steel, self-
winding mechanical movement
with date, two time zones,
and alarm

ABOVE RIGHT: **OFFICINE
PANERAI LUMINOR
AUTOMATIC CHRONO**, 1999,
white gold, self-winding
mechanical movement with
chronograph

OFFICINE PANERAI LUMINOR ARKTOS, 2004, stainless steel, self-winding mechanical movement with date

FAR RIGHT: **OFFICINE PANERAI LUMINOR SUBMERSIBLE**, c. 2000, stainless steel, self-winding mechanical movement with date; water-resistant to 1,000 meters

OFFICINE PANERAI LUMINOR TANTALIUM, 2003, tantalium, mechanical movement

OFFICINE PANERAI LUMINOR MARINA, 2002, yellow gold, self-winding mechanical movement with date

OFFICINE PANERAI LUMINOR BLACKSEAL, 2002, titanium, self-winding mechanical movement with date and concealed dial

Omega

Omega is one of the most renowned watch companies, having produced excellent watches since 1848 — although the name Omega didn't appear for another six decades. The company was first named after its founder, and later his sons as well — Louis Brandt et Fils. According to legend, the Brandts wanted their brand to be the last word in watchmaking, and eventually selected the final letter of the Greek alphabet as the company's name.

One of the largest pocket watchmakers in Switzerland, Omega was among the first companies to manufacture and promote wristwatches; before World War I its catalog already listed several wristwatches for men, including a chronograph.

The company was innovative and interesting; as early as 1892 it created the world's first minute-repeater wristwatch and had won numerous design competitions, as well as many observatory contests. As a result, it prospered into the 1920s, but the exigencies of the Depression and the fading demand for watches propelled Omega and Tissot to merge in 1930, form a company called SSIH. Eventually other brands were brought in as well, including Lemania, Rayville, Lanco, Cortebert, Marc Favre, and Hamilton, and SSIH was one of the companies that later formed the Swatch Group, which now owns Omega.

Some of Omega's great watches, past and present, include the Constellation, dating from 1952; the Seamaster, initially produced as a waterproof watch in 1948 and still one of Omega's most popular models; and the Speedmaster, which first appeared in 1957 and was NASA's pick to accompany astronauts into space (both Neil Armstrong and Buzz Aldrin wore Speedmasters on their lunar mission). It continues to be the mechanical watch of choice of the United States space program.

Recently, Omega bought from English master-watchmaker George Daniels a new innovation called the co-axial escapement. Considered by many to be the first practical new watch escapement of the last two centuries, it was designed to reduce internal friction and dependence on lubrication, thus requiring less frequent service. Omega is employing the co-axial escapement in an increasing number of its current lines, with the intention of outfitting all of its future mechanical watches with it. Time will tell if the invention becomes a new standard in watchmaking.

OMEGA CONSTELLATION GENEVA OBSERVATORY, 1952, yellow gold with cloisonné enamel dial, self-winding mechanical movement

OMEGA CONSTELLATION, 1960s, pink gold, self-winding mechanical movement with date. The so-called "pie-pan dial" of this watch is very attractive to collectors

OMEGA TISSOT WATCH CO., 1930s, stainless steel and pink gold, mechanical movement. This is an early attempt to waterproof a wristwatch

In a historical sense, Omega represents the cult of the workingman's watch. These timepieces were always well-made, basic watches known for being excellent timekeepers as well as being relatively easy to repair. Omega watches also won numerous awards in the chronometer trials, and the brand still holds the record for the single most accurate wristwatch ever rated in competition.

LEFT: **OMEGA CONSTELLATION,** c. 1969, yellow gold, self-winding mechanical movement with date. This is a "souscription" watch, so-called because the first watch for which Abraham-Louis Breguet solicited subsciptions was a simple single-handed model

OPPOSITE LEFT: **OMEGA 1894** (face and back), 1994, pink gold, mechanical movement

OPPOSITE RIGHT: **OMEGA CHRONOMÈTRE** (face and movement), 1940s, stainless steel, mechanical movement

OMEGA CONSTELLATION, 1970s, yellow gold, self-winding mechanical movement with day and date

OMEGA CONSTELLATION MEGAQUARTZ F 2.4 MHZ, 1970s, yellow gold, quartz movement with date

ABOVE: **OMEGA DE VILLE CO-AXIAL RATTRAPANTE,** 2006, platinum, self-winding co-axial mechanical movement with split-seconds chronograph and date

After a period of relative quiet, Omega has recommitted itself to mechanical chronometry by adopting master watchmaker George Daniels' co-axial escapement. Equally successful as an accuracy-enhacing feature and a marketing tool, Omega's co-axial escapement is considered to be the most significant innovation in escapement design in 250 years.

OMEGA DE VILLE, 1999, yellow gold, self-winding co-axial mechanical movement with date

OMEGA CONSTELLATION ELECTRONIC F300 HZ, 1970s, yellow gold, electronic movement with date

RIGHT: **OMEGA RANCHERO,** c. 1958, gold filled, mechanical movement

FAR RIGHT: **OMEGA SEAMASTER AQUA TERRA CHRONOMETER,** 2000s, stainless steel, self-winding co-axial mechanical movement with date

OMEGA SEAMASTER PLANET OCEAN, 2005, stainless steel, self-winding co-axial mechanical movement with date; water-resistant to 600 meters

The Seamaster is a very popular dive watch, easily recognizable for the eye-catching helium escape valve at ten o'clock. The helium is considered by many to be a necessary feature on any true divers watch as it allows saturation diving without the risk of explosive decompression. The new Planet Ocean with its bold retro styling is a very stylish addition to the Seamaster line.

OMEGA SPEEDMASTER PROFESSIONAL EYES ON THE STARS, 1990s, stainless steel, mechanical movement with chronograph

OMEGA SPEEDMASTER PROFESSIONAL, early 1960s, stainless steel, mechanical movement with chronograph

OMEGA SPEEDMASTER PROFESSIONAL, made in 1969–1972 to commemorate *Apollo XI*, yellow gold, mechanical movement with chronograph

OMEGA SEAMASTER CALGARY AND SEOUL, 1988, titanium and yellow gold, quartz movement with chronograph and date

OMEGA FLIGHTMASTER, 1974–75, yellow gold, mechanical movement with chronograph and two time zones

OMEGA SPEEDMASTER BROAD ARROW, c. 2000, stainless steel, mechanical movement with chronograph

Parmigiani Fleurier

Michel Parmigiani (b. 1950) is another of the talented young watchmakers who has set up his own shop and created a line of beautifully designed and well-made watches; however, he may be best known for refurbishing a watch known as the Montre Sympathique, originally crafted by Abraham-Louis Breguet, and for assisting on the reconstruction of Giovanni de Dondi's astronomical clock from the mid-fourteenth century.

Parmigiani first established a watchmaking repair and service company, but with an influx of capital in 1990 was able to devote himself to creating new timepieces.

The company was purchased by the Sandoz Foundation in 1996, and in 2003 the movement manufacturer Vaucher Manufacture Fleurier was spun off as a supplier of high-grade movements (a sizable percentage of which are supplied to Parmigiani).

Parmigiani has also played a critical role (alongside Chopard and Bovet) in establishing a Fleurier Quality (FQ) Foundation label, involving quality construction and finishing criteria similar to those needed to qualify for the Geneva Seal, but combined with an independent chronometer certification (COSC).

Parmigiani produces approximately a thousand watches each year; the company claims it takes four hundred hours to manufacture just one. So far, although it's a new company, Parmigiani models have been holding their own at auction.

LEFT: **PARMIGIANI FLEURIER FORMA**, c. 2000, white gold, self-winding mechanical movement with date

BELOW: **PARMIGIANI FLEURIER TORIC TOURBILLON**, 2000s, platinum, mechanical movement with tourbillon

PARMIGIANI FLEURIER IONICA TIMEPIECE IN HONOUR OF DR. DUCHENNE (unique piece), 2005, pink gold, mechanical movement with date and power-reserve indicator

RIGHT: **PARMIGIANI FLEURIER TORIC QUANTIÈME PERPETUEL RÉTROGRADE**, 2002, platinum, self-winding mechanical movement with perpetual calendar and moon-phase indicator

PARMIGIANI FLEURIER TORIC MINUTE REPEATER, c. 2000, platinum, mechanical movement with minute repeater

Patek Philippe

If there is any name that deserves top billing in the watch industry, it is Patek Philippe. It is the king, and shows no sign of relinquishing its throne.

Patek Philippe was founded in Geneva in 1839 by an exiled Polish nobleman, Count Antoni Norbert de Prawdzic (1811–1877), and his compatriot François Czapek (b. 1811). When the former became a Swiss citizen, he changed his name to Patek, ensuring that future watch lovers would be able to pronounce the name of their favorite brand.

The brand's first watches were signed Patek, Czapek & Co. However, in the mid-1840s, Czapek left the company after quarreling with Patek, and French watchmaker Jean Adrien Philippe (1815-1894) joined it. Philippe later became the inventor of the company's stem-winding and hand-setting mechanism, and in 1851, his name became part of the firm's.

Patek Philippe quickly became a leader in its field, introducing many technical improvements, including the sweep seconds hand; it also produced interesting and reliable complications, such as chronographs, perpetual calendars, and repeaters.

Patek Philippe also produced many remarkable custom-made watches for individual clients — including Americans Henry Graves and James Ward Packard — with as many as twenty-four complications. These pocket watches have garnered the highest prices ever at auction; the record is held by what's known as the Henry Graves Supercomplication, which sold at Sotheby's in 1999 for more than $11 million.

During the Depression, the company, like many others, did poorly, but was rescued when brothers Charles and Jean Stern acquired the majority of Patek Philippe shares; Stern family members still own and run the firm.

Shortly after World War II, Patek Philippe established an electronic division, and in the 1950s, the company pioneered quartz technology, filing several patents and winning multiple awards. The firm also produced high-end industrial and electronic timepieces that were installed in power stations, hospitals, airports, and other public buildings and factories.

Today Patek Philippe produces about thirty thousand watches a year; its most famous line, the Calatrava, dates from 1932.

The company continues to create some of the most remarkable complicated watches; it is unlikely that any other company can top Patek Philippe's high-end complications with ones that consistently work. True to its legacy, when Patek Philippe announces it will produce a supercomplicated watch, the rest of the watch world believes it.

Patek Philippe has always been shrewd in its approach to the vintage watch market. If your Patek is broken, the company will fix it for you no matter how old it is — even if the repairer has to make pinions and wheels that would never fit into any other watch. You will probably have to pay a considerable fee for this service, but not as much as you would for a new Patek.

Patek Philippe also runs the most beautiful watch museum in the industry. To stock it, the company purchased many of its old watches, a tactic which has also helped keep vintage prices high at auctions.

Patek Philippe is not the most innovative of watch companies, and it doesn't bend to fashion. Unlike most companies today, which produce ultra-large watches for a market that seems to believe bigger is better, Patek Philippe offers few models larger than thirty-eight millimeters. Perhaps this is because the company doesn't need to change with the times. Owning a Patek Philippe is unlike owning any other watch; there is no such thing as a low-quality Patek, and consumers bend to the company's wishes.

LEFT: **PATEK PHILIPPE CALATRAVA**, c. 1950, yellow gold, mechanical movement

OPPOSITE TOP LEFT: **PATEK PHILIPPE 10 DAYS REF. 5100J**, (back) 2000, yellow gold, mechanical movement with power-reserve indicator

OPPOSITE TOP RIGHT: **PATEK PHILIPPE CALATRAVA REF. 5053**, 2000s, pink gold, self-winding mechanical movement

OPPOSITE BOTTOM LEFT: **PATEK PHILIPPE CALATRAVA REF. 5000**, 2000s, rose gold, self-winding mechanical movement

OPPOSITE BOTTOM RIGHT: **PATEK PHILIPPE REF. 3878**, 1970s, yellow gold, self-winding mechanical movement

PATEK PHILIPPE CALATRAVA, 1940s, yellow gold, mechanical movement

YEAR 2000

PATEK PHILIPPE

GENEVE SWISS

TWENTY-
ADJUSTED
ISOCHRONISM

NINE (29) JEWELS
TO HEAT. COLD.
AND FIVE (5) POSITIONS

Nº 3201667

750

PPCo

PATEK PHILIPPE

ABOVE: **PATEK PHILIPPE CHRONOMETRO GONDOLO**, 1920s, yellow gold, mechanical movement

ABOVE: **PATEK PHILIPPE REF. 2440**, 1949, pink gold, mechanical movement

RIGHT: **PATEK PHILIPPE TOPOLINO REF. 2414**, c. 1949, yellow gold, mechanical movement

RIGHT: **PATEK PHILIPPE**, c. 1943, pink gold, mechanical movement

RIGHT: **PATEK PHILIPPE BANANA REF. 2442**, 1951, yellow gold, mechanical movement

RIGHT: **PATEK PHILIPPE TOP HAT REF. 1450**, c. 1946, yellow gold, mechanical movement

BELOW: **PATEK PHILIPPE TV REF. 2540**, c. 1955, yellow gold, self-winding mechanical movement

RIGHT: **PATEK PHILIPPE RAM'S HORNS REF. 2471**, c. 1957, pink gold, mechanical movement

RIGHT: **PATEK PHILIPPE HOURGLASS REF. 1593**, 1956, yellow gold, mechanical movement

LEFT: **PATEK PHILIPPE 150TH ANNIVERSARY JUMPING HOUR WATCH REF. 3969**, 1989, pink gold, mechanical movement

LEFT: **PATEK PHILIPPE**, 1992, platinum, self-winding mechanical movement with perpetual calendar and moon-phase display

2006 is the thirtieth anniversary of the Nautilus line, Patek's entry into the steel luxury sports-watch market. Designed by Gérald Genta, the watch was something of a sleeper for many years but is now enjoying increasing popularity.

RIGHT: **PATEK PHILIPPE AQUANAUT REF. 5066**, late 1990s, yellow gold, self-winding mechanical movement with date

RIGHT: **PATEK PHILIPPE NAUTILUS JUMBO REF. 3700/1**, 1976, stainless steel, self-winding mechanical movement with date

PATEK PHILIPPE REF. 3424, 1968, pink gold, mechanical movement

RIGHT: **PATEK PHILIPPE REF. 3412**, 1959, yellow gold, mechanical movement. This example is a prototype

A brand noted for its conservatism, Patek has nonetheless occasionally offered some surprisingly styled asymmetric and unusual pieces, including the three wristwatches on this page, designed by Gilbert Albert in the 1950s and 1960s.

PATEK PHILIPPE REF. 3422, 1961, yellow gold, mechanical movement

LEFT: **PATEK PHILIPPE**
REF. 2499, 1957, pink gold,
mechanical movement with
chronograph, perpetual
calendar, and moon-phase
indicator

Chronographs, particu-
larly with perpetual
calendars, and World
Time watches, are guar-
anteed to be top sellers.
They have achieved a
cult status of their own.

ABOVE: **PATEK PHILIPPE**, 1927,
yellow gold, mechanical
movement with chronograph

RIGHT: **PATEK PHILIPPE**
REF. 533, late 1930s, yellow
gold, mechanical movement
with chronograph

RIGHT: **PATEK PHILIPPE TV**
REF. 5020, c. 2000, yellow
gold, mechanical movement
with chronograph, perpetual
calendar, and moon-phase
indicator

ABOVE: **PATEK PHILIPPE THE CELESTIAL WRISTWATCH REF. 5102**, 2002, white gold, self-winding mechanical movement with mean solar time indicator, nocturnal sky chart of the Northern Hemisphere, moon phases and moon orbit indicators, and time of the meridian passage of Sirius and moon

LEFT: **PATEK PHILIPPE WORLD TIME REF. 1415**, 1941, yellow gold, mechanical movement with world time

PATEK PHILIPPE WORLD TIME REF. 5110, 2000, platinum, self-winding mechanical movement with world time

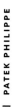

Piaget

Although Piaget is known as much for its jewelry as for its watches, the company has been producing ebauches for other watch brands, including Omega, Longines, Rolex, and Audemars Piguet, for more than a century.

Because few are aware of this fact, experts often refer to Piaget as "the best, least respected company in the business." Some may not take the company seriously, but Piaget has been making excellent watches and movements for longer than most brands have been in existence. Piagets have been making watches in Switzerland since the mid-nineteenth century; George-Édouard Piaget (1855–1931), the current company's founder, began producing them in 1874.

The company is probably most famous for its gold Polo watches, which were the ultimate lifestyles-of-the-rich-and-famous watches in the 1980s and have recently been reissued. Piaget's current design success is the Altiplano line, especially its unusual square, ultra-thin model.

Among Piaget's other accomplishments was the creation, in 1956, of the slimmest mechanical movement then made, which the company used successfully in both men's and women's models. (The company has long excelled at producing slim movements, having made high-quality ultra-thin movements as early as the mid-1920s.)

In 1988, Cartier acquired Piaget (along with Baume & Mercier, which Piaget had acquired twenty-three years earlier). Eleven years later the city of Venice commissioned Piaget to restore its famous San Marco Tower clock, completed in 1499 by Giampaolo Rainieri and his son, Giancarlo. Piaget's work was done by 1999, at which time Piaget issued a commemorative skeleton chronograph in blue and gold, the colors of Venice.

Piaget has been immortalized in pop culture as well; when the writers for the television show *Seinfeld* wanted to have an unseemly character shoplift a prestigious brand-name watch, they had her pick off a Piaget.

BELOW: **PIAGET EMPERADOR**, 2003, white gold, mechanical watch with tourbillon and moon-phase indicator

LEFT: **PIAGET**, 1990s, yellow gold, self-winding mechanical movement with perpetual calendar and moon-phase indicator

ABOVE: **PIAGET RECTANGLE À L'ANCIENNE XL**, 2005, pink gold, self-winding mechanical movement with date, retrograde seconds, and power-reserve indicator

Richard Mille

Watch designer Richard Mille (b. 1951), once the watch tsar of the French jewelry house Mauboussin, created his own company in 2001 and is capitalizing on the connections he established in the watchmaking community to realize his high-mech concepts (he has been a consultant for such companies as Audemars Piguet and Baccarat, and has family connections to the master complications makers Renaud & Papi). So far, his very expensive watches all have a characteristic tonneau case (his collaboration on a custom-made watch with Philippe Starck is an exception) and utilize cutting-edge materials often chosen for their light weight.

Although the brand is only five years old, it has made remarkable inroads in the luxury market. Two of the drivers of Mille's success: Formula One heavyweights such as Felipe Massa and Jean Todt can be seen showing off their Richard Mille timepieces to race fans around the world.

OPPOSITE: **RICHARD MILLE BY STARCK AUTOMATIC CALIBER RM 005-1** (unique piece), 2005, white gold, self-winding mechanical movement with date; case designed by Philippe Starck

LEFT: **RICHARD MILLE RM 004-V2**, 2000s, mechanical movement with split-seconds chronograph, and power-reserve, torque, and function indicators

ABOVE: **RICHARD MILLE RM 003** (front and back), 2003, white gold, mechanical movement with tourbillon, two time zones, and power-reserve and torque indicators

LEFT: **RICHARD MILLE RM 009 FELIPE MASSA** (front and back), 2000s, ALUSIC (Aluminum AS7G-Silicum-Carbide), mechanical movement with tourbillon

Roger Dubuis

The Swiss-born Roger Dubuis (b. 1940) spent fourteen years at Patek Philippe as a specialist in complicated timepieces. Then, in 1980, he became an independent watchmaker, restoring antique collectors' timepieces, developing projects for major brands, and researching what eventually became his specialty: retrograde complications.

Working with partner Carlos Dias, Dubuis introduced his first watches in 1995; today the company has almost 150 employees producing many different models, each limited to only twenty-eight watches.

Roger Dubuis is no longer with the company, but the firm continues to produce oversized, well-finished, retro designs. Among its models are the GoldenSquare, 43 by 43 millimeters, and the MuchMore-series watches, which are often even bigger. The brand is also introducing a new line of sports watches with finely finished movements. These watches are expensive, flamboyant, and so far, have done unusually well at auction compared with other new brands. The company has built a very large factory in Geneva, and it is already expanding.

ROGER DUBUIS BI-RETROGRADE CALENDAR, 2000, white gold, mechanical movement with day and date and moon-phase indicator

ROGER DUBUIS EASY DIVER – JUST FOR FRIENDS, 2004, stainless steel, self-winding mechanical movement; water resistant to 300 meters

ROGER DUBUIS HOMMAGE BIRETROGRADE PERPETUAL CALENDAR, late 1990s, yellow gold, mechanical movement with perpetual calendar and moon-phase indicator

ROGER DUBUIS HOMMAGE BIRETROGRADE PERPETUAL CALENDAR CHRONOGRAPH, 1990s, white gold, mechanical movement with chronograph, perpetual calendar, and moon-phase indicator

ROGER DUBUIS MUCHMORE, 2001, white gold, self-winding mechanical movement with day and date and moon-phase indicator

RIGHT: **ROGER DUBUIS GOLD
AND SQUARE**, C. 2000, white
gold with diamonds,
mechanical movement with
tourbillon, date, and power-
reserve indicator

BELOW: **ROGER DUBUIS
TOOMUCH**, 2002, pink gold,
mechanical movement

Rolex

Ask the average person on the street to name a good watch, and nine out of a ten will say Rolex. Few brands stand out as powerfully in their field. On any given day on eBay there may be a hundred Audemars Piguets or three hundred Pateks for sale, but there will be more than four thousand Rolexes.

Rolex was established by Hans Wilsdorf (1881–1960), who was born in Germany but moved to Switzerland in 1900, where he became interested in watches. He then took a position with a London-based company importing watches and married an Englishwoman.

Although the pocket watch was still the preeminent timepiece for men, Wilsdorf decided that the future belonged to the wristwatch, and so he created a London-based company called Wilsdorf & Davis to import watches (Davis was his brother-in-law). Within a few years, the company was one of the foremost watch merchants in the United Kingdom. Wilsdorf next wanted to create an outstanding brand to compete with the others he was already selling. It is said he chose the name Rolex because, while he was sitting on a bus, it suddenly occurred to him that "rolex" was the sound of a watch being wound. (Yet another version of the legend is that the name is an amalgam of *horlogerie exquise*, or "exquisite watchmaking.")

At the time, few pocket-watch manufacturers were producing small movements that were accurate and reliable enough to fit inside a wristwatch. The Swiss company Aegler agreed to supply Wilsdorf with movements. In 1914, the new brand won the first chronometer certification ever given to a wristwatch. After World War I, when an import tax increase of 33 percent made the Swiss movements prohibitively expensive, Rolex moved to Switzerland; in 1920 Montres Rolex S.A. was founded in Geneva.

Because watches were easily damaged by dust and moisture, Wilsdorf developed a revolutionary screw-down crown and caseback mechanism, and in 1926 he introduced the Rolex Oyster, a highly accurate, waterproof watch. (Wilsdorf came up with the name in honor of the work it takes to pry open the shell of an actual oyster.)

When Wilsdorf heard that an English secretary named Mercedes Gleitze was planning to swim the English Channel,

he asked her to wear an Oyster. The watch worked as well when Gleitze emerged on shore as when she'd first entered the water. Wilsdorf then made sure that stores selling Rolexes featured aquariums in their windows, all holding submerged Rolexes. The campaigns paid off. The name Rolex became synonymous with dependability.

New models and innovations followed. In 1931 came the Perpetual, a self-winding watch powered by the movement of the wearer's arm, based on technology developed by Harwood that Wilsdorf purchased; in 1945, the company introduced the Datejust, the first wristwatch to show the date magnified two and a half times by a lens; less than a decade later Rolex followed with the Day-Date.

Wilsdorf's great gift was his foresight. He bet on the wristwatch very early and each of his major innovations (putting the timepiece on the wrist, making it accurate, making it waterproof, and making it automatic) helped create the modern wristwatch as we know it. When Hans Wilsdorf died in 1960, his estate established the Hans Wilsdorf Foundation, making Rolex a not-for-profit company.

Rolex continues to make high-quality, dependable watches. The downside for some is that the design of these watches changes less than most brands — a 2000 Datejust resembles one from thirty years ago. And the company doesn't produce a wide variety of interesting complications; there is no Rolex tourbillon, no ten-complication Rolex. Instead, the company's strength lies in its research and its engineering. Rolex continually upgrades its products from a purely functional standpoint, with no fanfare. These are superb mechanical watches for people who don't know anything about mechanical watches.

If you can't afford a Rolex, think about Tudor, its sister brand. Over the years Rolex tried many second lines, including Marconi, Unicorn, Rolco, and H. Wilsdorf, but none lasted except Tudor. Tudor does not use Rolex movements, instead opting for less expensive ones from ETA (although a proprietary Tudor movement is reportedly on the horizon). But its cases are the same, its designs are often similar, and its reputation for quality is very high.

ROLEX OYSTER PERPETUAL REF. 3131, 1940s, pink gold, self-winding mechanical movement

Hans Wilsdorf realized that chronometer certification would help convince a wary public of the accuracy of Rolex's products, and he used successful results to create legend. At one point, people suspected Rolex was fabricating test results because no wristwatches had ever been certified to such high degrees of accuracy before. This extremely rare Kew A certified wristwatch, right, is a case in point.

ROLEX OYSTER PERPETUAL REF. 5011/5015, 1950s, yellow gold, self-winding mechanical movement

ABOVE: **ROLEX OYSTER PERPETUAL DAY-DATE REF. 1803**, 1966, yellow gold, self-winding mechanical movement with date

ROLEX OYSTER PERPETUAL DATE REF. 1530, 1970s, stainless steel, self-winding mechanical movement with date

LEFT: **ROLEX OYSTER OBSERVATORY CHRONO-METER "KEW A" CERTIFICATE**, 1954, yellow gold, self-winding mechanical movement

FROM LEFT TO RIGHT:

ROLEX PRINCE BRANCARD REF. 971U, 1930, sterling silver, mechanical movement

ROLEX PRINCE ULTRA PRIMA REF. 3362, c. 1935, pink gold, mechanical movement

ROLEX PRINCE BRANCARD TIGER STRIPE REF. 971, 1929, white and yellow gold, mechanical movement

ROLEX PRINCE SUPER PRÉCISION AERODYNAMIC REF. 3361, launched at the 1939 Swiss National Exhibition in Zurich, produced in the 1940s, yellow gold, mechanical movement

RIGHT: **ROLEX OYSTER PERPETUAL RIGID HOODED REF. 3599**, 1940s, stainless steel, self-winding mechanical movement

BELOW: **ROLEX OYSTER PERPETUAL**, c. 1933, yellow gold, self-winding mechanical movement

The Prince, introduced in 1928, was one of Rolex's most beautifully designed watches of all time. The line was resuscitated in 2006, and it is the first Rolex to feature a display back.

ROLEX OYSTER, late 1920s, pink gold, mechanical movement

ROLEX OYSTER, REF. 678, 1935, yellow gold, mechanical movement

Rolex enjoyed three big coups in the watchmaking business: accuracy, water resistance, and self-winding. Screwdown crowns and backs made early Oysters more water resistant.

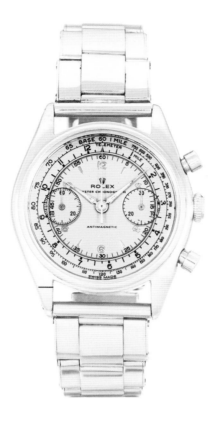

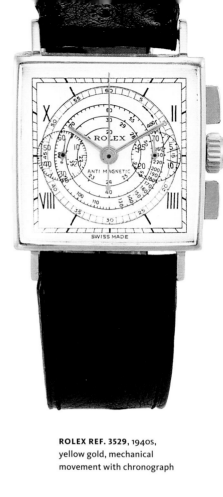

**ROLEX OYSTER JEAN-CLAUDE
KILLY REF. 4767**, 1940s,
stainless steel, mechanical
movement with chronograph
and triple-date calendar

**ROLEX OYSTER MONOBLOCCO
REF. 4500**, 1946, pink gold,
mechanical movement with
chronograph

ROLEX REF. 3529, 1940s,
yellow gold, mechanical
movement with chronograph

Rolex's chronographs
are remarkably collect-
ible despite the fact that
the company used
outsourced movements
before 2000.

**ROLEX OYSTER MONOBLOCCO
REF. 4500**, mid-1940s,
stainless steel and pink gold,
mechanical movement with
chronograph

FAR RIGHT: **ROLEX PICCOLINO
REF. 3055**, 1930s, yellow gold,
mechanical movement with
chronograph

FAR LEFT: **ROLEX OYSTER PERPETUAL EXPLORER REF. 6610**, 1957, stainless steel, self-winding mechanical movement

LEFT: **ROLEX OYSTER PERPETUAL GMT-MASTER REF. 1675**, late 1950s, yellow gold, self-winding mechanical movement with date and twenty-four-hour hand

Collectors are particularly passionate about Rolex sports models, which have long been associated with explorers, adventurers, and athletes. In addition to the famous James Bond Submariner, an early version of the GMT was worn by Chuck Yeager as well as several astronauts. Rolex supplied GMTs to Pan Am pilots, helping to seal their reputation as serious pilots' watches

ROLEX OYSTER PERPETUAL DATE GMT-MASTER II REF. 16710, c. 2000, self-winding mechanical movement with date and two time zones

ROLEX OYSTER PERPETUAL DATE EXPLORER II REF. 1655, 1970s, stainless steel, self-winding mechanical movement with date and twenty-four-hour hand

**ROLEX OYSTER PERPETUAL
SUBMARINER REF. 5513**, 1972,
self-winding mechanical
movement; water-resistant to
200 meters

Introduced in 1960, the Rolex Daytona
may well be the most difficult to acquire
mass-produced wristwatch in production
today. Its cult status is due in part to
its historic affiliation with racing and the
desirability of the exotic Paul Newman
dial. The watch above is called the
"Pre-Daytona," produced in the late 1940s.
The rest of the watches on this page are
Daytonas produced since the 1960s.
The more recent editions are automatics.
An example of the first model (Ref. 6239)
is seen center row, right.

Seiko

Many watch fans assume this Japanese company is a product of the quartz revolution, but Seiko has been in business since the 1880s. Founded by Kintaro Hattori (1860–1934), the company was first a retail store in Tokyo, then a clock manufacturer, and later a maker of pocket watches and alarm clocks (the Japanese word *seikosha* means precision). Just as World War I was starting, Hattori decided that the company should begin manufacturing wristwatches. It did but continued to make other timekeeping devices.

Seiko's mechanical wristwatch movements initially copied Swiss movements, but its watchmakers soon began to innovate, developing a very simple and efficient automatic winding system called the Magic Lever, as well as one of the world's first automatic chronographs.

When Bulova came out with its Accutron at the end of the 1950s, Seiko also looked into new wristwatch technologies; with foresight, it opted for quartz rather than the electronic tuning fork (Seiko already had been making quartz clocks for some time). Seiko entered its quartz timekeeper in the Swiss chronometer competitions at Neuchâtel and then Geneva for only five years total, but in that short time went from 144th to 1st place overall in the final observatory competition held in Geneva in 1968. At the end of 1969, its quartz Astron, the first mass-produced quartz wristwatch, went on sale in Japan.

In 1969, Seiko perfected the vertical clutch chronograph, a device that made chronograph mechanisms simpler and more reliable, while simultaneously improving their

performance. Invented, but never fully developed, by the Swiss company Pierce, it was ignored for years by the Swiss brands, but in 1988 Piguet emulated it; eventually, Rolex, Omega, and Jaeger-LeCoultre did as well.

Continuing Seiko's technological achievements were the first computer wristwatch, appearing in 1984, and the Kinetic AGS, marketed in 1994 as a "quartz watch without a battery" — the wearer's movements generated the electricity needed to run the watch, just as an automatic mechanical watch generates power from the wearer.

The company's more recent groundbreaking wristwatch technologies include the Spring Drive mechanical movements with quartz regulators (available in both manual-wind and automatic versions) and the soon-to-be-released E-Paper watches, featuring a revolutionary, thin, flexible alternative to LCD with dramatic contrast for improved visibility.

Historically inexpensive, but often offering the reliability and accuracy of watches costing many times more, Seiko is a brand given short shrift among collectors in the West, although its dive watches have a certain cachet. Seiko compounds the situation by marketing its high-end lines only in Japan. The new Spring Drive is the first high-end Seiko to be sold in the rest of the world.

RIGHT: **SEIKO SUS SCFF001**, stainless steel, self-winding mechanical movement with date

FAR RIGHT: **SEIKO PROSPEX FLIGHTMASTER SBDS001**, titanium, self-winding mechanical movement with chronograph, date, and power-reserve indicator

ABOVE: **SEIKO PROSPEX KINETIC CHRONOGRAPH SBDV001**, 2003. titanium, self-winding electro-mechanical movement with chronograph and date

RIGHT: **SEIKO PROSPEX LANDMASTER SBDX007**, titanium, self-winding mechanical movement with date

ABOVE: **SEIKO PROSPEX 1000M PROFESSIONAL QUARTZ DIVER SSBS018**, quartz movement with date; water resistant to 1,000 meters

RIGHT: **SEIKO PROSPEX SBDA005**, titanium, self-winding mechanical movement with date; water resistant to 200 meters

BELOW: **SEIKO MARINEMASTER SBDX001**, stainless steel, self-winding mechanical movement with date; water resistant to 300 meters

BELOW: **SEIKO MARINEMASTER SPRING DRIVE SBDB001**, 2005, titanium, electro-mechanical movement with date, two time zones, and power-reserve indicator; water resistant to 600 meters

Sinn

This forty-year-old company is known for its chronographs. Like Breitling, whose watches Sinn products occasionally resemble, the firm constructs instruments for the wrist for professional pilots and divers — and people who dream of flying planes and undersea adventure.

Helmut Sinn (b. 1916), the company's founder, was, in fact, a pilot and flight instructor; hence designs that incorporate features resembling those of an airplane's instrument panel. In 1994, Sinn sold the company to IWC veteran Lothar Schmidt, who has developed watches that can work well under extreme conditions, few of which the average wearer will ever encounter, including high and low pressure and altitude, intense heat and cold, magnetic interference, and submergence in liquids. Schmidt's interest in innovation has spurred the brand to invest in new technologies, including argon-filled watches, super-hard stainless steel cases, and lubrication-free DIAPAL escapements.

LEFT: **SINN MODEL 756**, stainless steel, self-winding mechanical movement with chronograph and date

RIGHT: **SINN MODEL 142 TI D1**, stainless steel, self-winding mechanical movement with chronograph, day and date, and two time zones

RIGHT: **SINN MODEL U1,** 2005, stainless steel, self-winding mechanical movement with date; water-resistant to 1,000 meters

FAR RIGHT: **SINN MODEL EZM2,** stainless steel, self-winding mechanical movement with date; water resistant to 500 meters

LEFT: **SINN MODEL 356 FLIEGER II**, stainless steel, self-winding mechanical movement with chronograph, and day and date

RIGHT: **SINN MODEL 144 GMT CARGO**, stainless steel, self-winding mechanical movement with chronograph, date, and two time zones

LEFT: **SINN MODEL 900**, stainless steel, self-winding mechanical movement with chronograph, date, and two time zones

RIGHT: **SINN MODEL 203 ARKTIS**, stainless steel, self-winding mechanical movement with chronograph, and day and date; water-resistant to 300 meters. This watch was designed to withstand temperatures ranging from -50F to +175F.

Swatch

Swatch is the Swiss mouse that roared. In 1978, ETA, the movement division of the watch company SMH, was determined to create a better and slimmer quartz movement than the contemporary Japanese models. The Japanese were winning the race for market dominance, as mechanical watches lost favor and the Swiss lost jobs — employment dropped from more than ninety thousand people in sixteen hundred companies to about thirty thousand people in three hundred companies.

ETA succeeded: The movement, just under two millimeters tall, was the thinnest quartz movement ever produced; it made its first appearance as the Concord Delirium model, although Eterna and Longines also launched their own versions.

These models were not cheap, however, so the decision was made to compete with the Japanese in price as well as slimness. By the early 1980s the watch that eventually became the Swatch was developed. It was an inexpensive, all-plastic quartz watch in which the case's inside back was also its main plate.

The key to the Swatch watch's success was keeping these products from looking cheap — they had to be inexpensive yet stylish. And they had to come in a variety of colors.

In 1983, the first watches marketed as Swatches were introduced, and they were immediately successful; within two years, more than ten million had been produced. From then on, the company introduced new models and designs every year; nearly all were well received and went on to sell millions more. Soon Swatch was producing chronographs and even non-quartz models. Designers such as Vivienne Westwood and Studio Azzurro created models, as did Yoko Ono, Micha Klein, Victor Vasarely, Kiki Picasso, Keith Haring, Irit Batsry, and Pedro Almodóvar.

By the mid-1990s the watches were being made in materials other than plastic; some now came in steel, aluminum, and in interesting metal combinations.

Swatch continued to innovate. Newer models, such as the Swatch Access, contain an antenna and a microchip and can serve as ski-lift tickets or company time cards; the Swatch Paparazzi is an MSN Direct wrist-computer that can download everything from news flashes to movie showtimes, horoscopes, and weather reports directly to one's wrist.

Today Swatch sells more than twenty-five million watches a year, constantly introducing new models and designs; some have become collectors' items, especially those in its Irony series.

SWATCH STANDARD GENTS JELLY FISH, 1985, plastic, quartz movement

This now-huge company has a tortuous history, beginning with the amalgamation of two groups of Swiss companies — SSIH, founded in 1930 with the union of Omega and Tissot, and ASUAG (Allgemeine Schweizerische Uhrenindustrie AG), founded in 1931. SSIH was formed because so many Swiss companies were suffering during the Depression, and unification seemed the best antidote to bankruptcy. Slowly SSIH managed to take over several brands that might otherwise have gone under, and the amalgamation prospered.

ASUAG, on the other hand, was created to develop and promote the Swiss watch industry; it was composed mostly of movement companies and other behind-the-scenes firms. Then, when both unions faced trouble in the 1970s during the quartz scare, the company asked Nicolas Hayek (b. 1928), currently chairman of the board and chief executive officer of Swatch, for advice; he recommended the companies merge and create a low-cost product to compete with the Japanese models. In 1983 ASUAG and SSIH became ASUAG-SSIH, which was later shortened to SMH; in 1998 it was renamed the Swatch Group. Among the company's holdings are the brands Breguet, Blancpain, Glashütte Original, Jaquet Droz, Omega, Longines, Rado, Union Glashütte, Tissot, Calvin Klein, and Hamilton.

FAR LEFT: **SWATCH STANDARD GENTS GN701**, 1983, plastic, quartz movement with day and date

LEFT: **SWATCH SPECIAL KIKI**, 1985, plastic, quartz movement; designed by Kiki Picasso

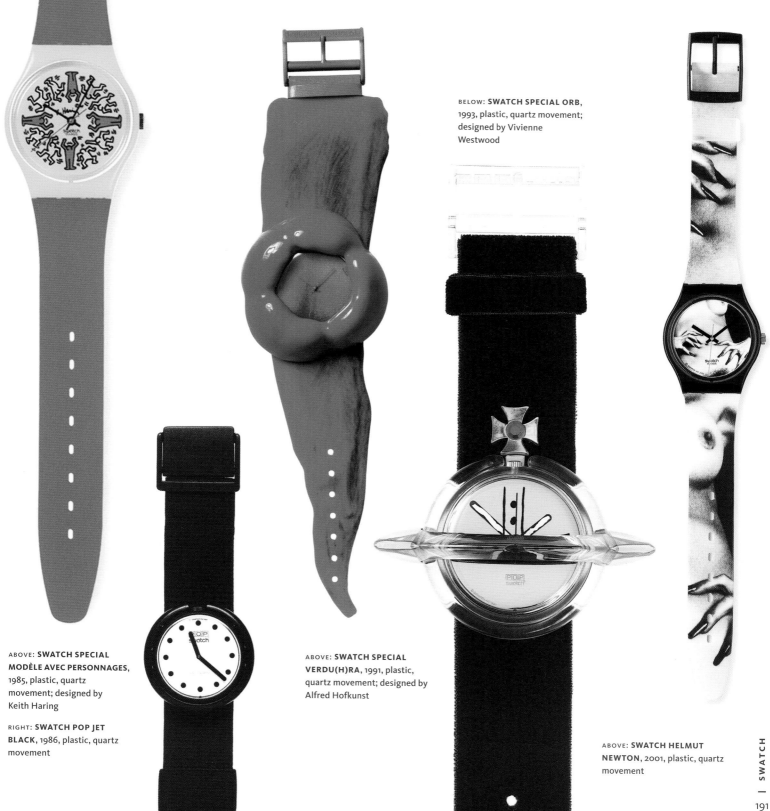

ABOVE: **SWATCH SPECIAL MODÈLE AVEC PERSONNAGES**, 1985, plastic, quartz movement; designed by Keith Haring

RIGHT: **SWATCH POP JET BLACK**, 1986, plastic, quartz movement

ABOVE: **SWATCH SPECIAL VERDU(H)RA**, 1991, plastic, quartz movement; designed by Alfred Hofkunst

BELOW: **SWATCH SPECIAL ORB**, 1993, plastic, quartz movement; designed by Vivienne Westwood

ABOVE: **SWATCH HELMUT NEWTON**, 2001, plastic, quartz movement

RIGHT: **SWATCH SPECIAL
PLUME DE FETE**, 2001, plastic,
quartz movement

SWATCH POP HOT STUFF,
1995, plastic, quartz movement

SWATCH SKIN SWEET PLANET,
2004, plastic, quartz
movement

**SWATCH TOUCH BUNNY-
SUTRA**, 2004, plastic, quartz
movement with erotic game
function

**SWATCH BEAT PLASTIC
NET-TIME**, 1999, plastic, quartz
movement with chronograph,
date, alarm, and two time zones

SWATCH IRONY RENVERSÉ, 1995, base metal, quartz movement

SWATCH SQUARE TYPICAL SQUARE, 2000, plastic, quartz movement

SWATCH AUTOMATIC BLUE MATIC, 1991, plastic, self-winding mechanical movement

SWATCH SKIN BLACK OUT TOO, 1997, plastic, quartz movement

SWATCH IRONY BLACK SCEPTRE, 2002, stainless steel, quartz movement with date

SWATCH DIAPHANE ONE – VENDÔME, 2001, translucent plastic, aluminium, diamond, sapphire, and ruby, mechanical movement with revolving escapement

SWATCH TRESOR MAGIQUE, 1993, platinum, self-winding mechanical movement

SWATCH BEAT ALUMEDIUM DOUBLE DOT, 2001, quartz movement with chronograph, date, alarm, and two time zones; water-resistant to 100 meters

LEFT: **SWATCH IRONY SCUBA**, 1998, aluminum, quartz movement; water-resistant to 200 meters

RIGHT: **SWATCH SKYRIDER**, 2002, plastic, quartz movement with chronograph and date

RIGHT: **SWATCH SKINCHRONO ON THE ROAD**, 2004, plastic, quartz movement with chronograph

BELOW: **SWATCH BEAT PAPARAZZI URBAN NEWS CAB**, 2004, quartz movement with chronograph, date, alarm, and two time zones

ABOVE: **SWATCH IRONY HIGH TAIL**, 1996, aluminum, quartz movement with chronograph

LEFT: **SWATCH CHRONO CLASSIC BROWN**, 1990, plastic, quartz movement with chronograph

TAG Heuer

This is another company that has long been renowned for its chronographs; in fact, many of them were once manufactured for other quality brands, such as Rolex.

Founder Édouard Heuer (1840–1892) was an innovator and inventor, and the company (which started around 1860) continued his legacy for more than a century, creating excellent (often custom-made) timepieces for professionals. In 1916, for instance, the company created the Microsplit, a stopwatch that was able to time events to a hundredth of a second. The official timekeeper of several Olympic Games, Heuer profited greatly from its line of stopwatches and other racing-related timepieces.

Heuer was especially successful in the United States, particularly after it bought the popular Swiss-based Jules Jürgensen brand.

Through the 1960s and 1970s, Heuer continued to innovate, finding successes with a quartz timer and with watches featuring both analog and digital displays on their dials. Heuer also enjoyed great success with its Carrera line of chronographs (started in 1963). Vintage Heuer chronographs from the 1950s to the 1970s are widely collected.

However, in the late 1970s, the company faltered. It had already merged with Leonidas, another Swiss company, and then was sold to Lemania, at that time a division of Piaget; Lemania helped reorganize the company but soon sold it to the TAG group — and thus its new name, TAG Heuer. (Today the company is owned by LVMH.)

Although the company has produced many well-known models, its most famous is the Monaco chronograph, worn by Steve McQueen in the film *Le Mans* in 1971. The watch has recently been reissued and is a bestseller for the company. Its Kirium line has also been highly profitable.

Recently Heuer announced it will produce a highly innovative line called the V4, featuring a belt-driven movement.

TOP: **HEUER BUNDESWEHR CHRONOGRAPH**, 1960s, stainless steel, mechanical movement with chronograph

ABOVE: **TAG HEUER AQUA-GRAPH**, c. 2000, stainless steel, self-winding mechanical movement with chronograph, water-resistant to 500 meters

OPPOSITE: **TAG HEUER CALIBRE 360 CHRONOGRAPH** (prototype), 2005, titanium, self-winding belt-driven mechanical movement with chronograph, 1/100th second diablotine, power-reserve indicator, and 10-minute register

HEUER, 1950s, stainless steel, mechanical movement with chronograph

HEUER MONZA, c. 2000, stainless steel, self-winding mechanical movement with chronograph and date

HEUER CARRERA, c. 2000, stainless steel, mechanical movement with chronograph and date

TAG HEUER MONACO, 1990s, yellow gold, self-winding mechanical movement with chronograph and date

ABOVE: **TAG HEUER MONACO**, 1990s, stainless steel, self-winding mechanical movement with chronograph and date

RIGHT: **HEUER MONACO**, 1970s, stainless steel, self-winding mechanical movement with chronograph and date

Ulysse Nardin

Watchmaker Ulysse Nardin (1823–1876) founded his company in 1846. Sixteen years later, at the London International Exhibition, Nardin received the Prize Medal (the highest honor) in the category of "complicated watches, pocket chronometers." This award placed the watchmaker in the lead among pocket chronometer makers; his company continued to win many awards, even after the senior Nardin died and his son, Paul-David, took over. In 1915, at the Naval Observatory in Washington D.C., Ulysse Nardin took first place among sixty marine chronometers; seven years later, at the same trials, Ulysse Nardin marine chronometers again captured first place — and second and third as well.

Like so many other Swiss companies, Ulysse Nardin struggled during the 1970s; in 1983 it was rescued by former Jaeger-LeCoultre executive Rolf W. Schnyder.

Although its output today includes chronometers, chronographs, and large-date watches, Ulysse Nardin also creates many unusual timepieces, reflecting the astronomical interests of its great watchmaker, Dr. Ludwig Oechslin. Fascinated by the subject, Oechslin created a series of watches called the Trilogy of Time; these watches include the Tellurium Johannes Kepler, the Astrolabium Galileo Galilei, and the Planetarium Copernicus — watches that go beyond telling time and indicate the positions of heavenly bodies.

Another recent marvel is the Freak — also designed by Oechslin — which turns conventional movement wisdom on its head. The watch looks like no other — essentially, it has neither hands nor dial nor crown, and it uses an escapement that doesn't need lubrication. Oechslin's newest creations also include the innovative Sonata wrist-alarm with dual time zones, the first such timepiece with an alarm that sounds like a minute repeater, and the Freak II, highlighted by yet another completely new escapement design.

LEFT: **ULYSSE NARDIN SAN MARCO HOUR STRIKER,** 1990s, platinum, self-winding mechanical movement with hour repeater and hour striking en passant

ABOVE: **ULYSSE NARDIN SAN MARCO USS CONSTITUTION,** 1990s, platinum with cloisonné enamel dial, self-winding mechanical movement

RIGHT: **ULYSSE NARDIN SAN MARCO CRISTOFORO COLOMBO — SANTA MARIA,** 1992, yellow gold with cloisonné enamel dial, self-winding mechanical movement

LEFT: **ULYSSE NARDIN TELLURIUM J. KEPLER**, 1992, platinum, self-winding mechanical movement with perpetual calendar, showing the rotation of the earth, sunrise and sunset, equinoxes, and eclipses of the sun and moon

RIGHT: **ULYSSE NARDIN PLANETARIUM COPERNICUS**, 1988, yellow gold, self-winding mechanical movement with perpetual calendar indicating months, the signs of the zodiac, and the astronomical positions of the planets in relation to the sun and the earth

ABOVE: **ULYSSE NARDIN ASTROLABIUM G. GALILEI**, 1985, white and yellow gold, self-winding mechanical movement with perpetual calendar and astrolabe indicating the position of the sun, the moon, and certain stars; sunrise and sunset; moon phases, moonrise, and moonset; and eclipses of the sun and moon

The company's gift for complicated astronomical displays are evidenced in Ludwig Oechslin's Trilogy of Time, consisting of homages to Copernicus, Kepler, and Galileo.

LEFT: **ULYSSE NARDIN**, 1950s, stainless steel, mechanical movement with chronograph and triple-date calendar

RIGHT: **ULYSSE NARDIN**, 1930s, yellow gold, mechanical movement with chronograph

OPPOSITE, TOP LEFT: **ULYSSE NARDIN MARINE CHRONOGRAPH**, 2000s. stainless steel, self-winding mechanical movement with chronograph and date

OPPOSITE, TOP RIGHT: **ULYSSE NARDIN ULYSSE I**, 2000s, rose gold, self-winding mechanical movement with date and power-reserve indicator

OPPOSITE, BOTTOM LEFT: **ULYSSE NARDIN SONATA CATHEDRAL DUAL TIME**, 2000s, rose gold, self-winding mechanical movement with date, alarm, and two time zones

OPPOSITE, BOTTOM RIGHT: **ULYSSE NARDIN MARINE CHRONOMETER 1846**, 2004, stainless steel, self-winding mechanical movement with date and power-reserve indicator

LEFT: **ULYSSE NARDIN**, 1930s, yellow gold, mechanical movement with chronograph

ULYSSE NARDIN ACQUA PERPETUAL, 2000s, stainless steel, self-winding mechanical movement with perpetual calendar

Ulysse Nardin owes much of its cachet among collectors to the genius of designer Ludwig Oechslin. His revolutionary GMT ± Perpetual has the first perpetual-calendar mechanism driven entirely by gears and wheels, making it simpler and more robust, as well as facilitating the adjustment of the time and date both forward and backward.

ULYSSE NARDIN GMT ± PERPETUAL, 2000s, pink gold, self-winding mechanical movement with perpetual calendar and two time zones

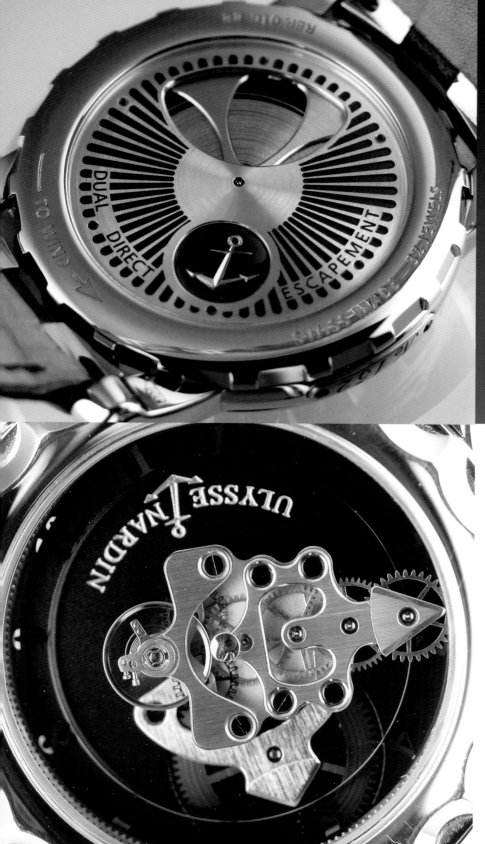

THIS PAGE: **FREAK**, 2001, white gold, mechanical movement with tourbillon

The Freak shows two other aspects of Oechslin's talent — the revolutionary approach of making the entire mechanism into a rotating display, coupled with a completely original escapement.

Universal Genève

Once one of the great watch companies, this older concern, founded in 1894, is known for its superb chronographs of the 1940s and 1950s, especially Compax models. When these watches appear at auction they command excellent prices, in part because the company was one of the most detail oriented and technologically advanced of its time.

Another great Universal watch was the Polerouter; many of these featured the company's highly praised micro-rotor movements. Designed in 1954 by a young Gérald Genta, it was the watch SAS pilots wore when flying over the North Pole on their route between California and Scandinavia.

In the late 1940s and 1950s, Universal Genève sold more watches than any other Swiss brand; however, the company faltered in later decades. In the 1970s, the company was bought by Bulova, and in 1986 it ended up in the hands of Stelux, a Hong Kong–based real estate and investment group. Today it is reissuing many of its former designs, but the company has yet to reclaim its former glory.

ABOVE: **UNIVERSAL GENÈVE AÉRO-COMPAX**, 1940s, stainless steel, mechanical movement with chronograph and two time zones

LEFT: **UNIVERSAL GENÈVE COMPAX**, 1940s, pink gold, mechanical movement with chronograph

UNIVERSAL GENÈVE UNI-COMPAX, 1950s, stainless steel, mechanical movement with chronograph

**UNIVERSAL GENÈVE
AÉRO-COMPAX**, 1940s,
stainless steel, mechanical
movement with chronograph
and two time zones

**UNIVERSAL GENÈVE
TRI-COMPAX**, early 1950s,
stainless steel, mechanical
movement with triple-date
calendar and moon-phase
indicator

**UNIVERSAL GENÈVE
MEDICO-COMPAX**, 1950s, pink
gold, mechanical movement
with chronograph

The term tri-Compax,
now used generally by
collectors to describe
watch faces with three
subdials, was originated
by Universal for its line
of chronographs in the
mid-twentieth century.

LEFT: **UNIVERSAL GENÈVE
COMPAX**, 1950s, yellow gold,
mechanical movement with
chronograph

Vacheron Constantin

Founded by watchmaker Jean-Marc Vacheron (1731–1805) in 1755, this company claims to be the oldest continually active watch manufacturer. Vacheron's reputation quickly grew, and by the 1770s he was making watches for Europe's royal courts. In 1785, Vacheron's son Abraham took over the company, which was prospering despite the ups and downs of French politics.

By the time Napoleon had been vanquished, Vacheron's grandson, Jaques-Barthélemy, was in charge; in need of capital, he asked François Constantin, the son of a wealthy grain merchant, to join the firm in 1819 — hence its new name, Vacheron & Constantin.

In 1839, Georges-Auguste Leschot joined the company. Leschot had been experimenting with machines that made interchangeable parts, leading to serial production of watch components, then a revolutionary concept that was ridiculed by the watchmaking establishment. At the time, watch parts were generally rough cut, formed, and finished by hand; in essence, every piece was custom-made. Because of Leschot's cost-saving inventions, including a turning and drilling machine that could consistently drill holes in exactly the same position, Vacheron & Constantin was soon able to sell high-quality watches at a lower price than that of other comparable brands. Karl Marx refers to Vacheron & Constantin in his treatise *Das Kapital*, noting its successful introduction of machines into the watchmaking process.

Several Vacheron & Constantin heirs took over the company following François Constantin's death; these included two women, Laure Vacheron-Pernessin and Catherine-Étienne Vacheron, the eighty-eight-year-old widow of Jaques-Barthélemy Vacheron, who led the company into the twentieth century.

In 1877, the name of the firm was officially registered as "Vacheron & Constantin, Fabricants, Genève"; three years later, the company began using the Maltese cross as its trademark. Then, in 1887, following the death of the two Vacheron women, the firm became a public company. It had its ups and downs, yet managed to produce some remarkable pocket watches, including one presented to King Fouad I of Egypt that was ultra-complicated.

In 1936, Charles Constantin became president, marking the first time that a Constantin had led the company since the mid-1850s. But the onset of World War II devastated sales, and in 1940 Georges Ketterer acquired a majority ownership position. He proved to be a solid leader, and the company prospered once more. In 1987, following Ketterer's death, the company once again changed hands. Today it is owned by Richemont and known as Vacheron Constantin (having dropped the ampersand in the late 1970s — some say Bell & Ross subsequently picked it up).

Vacheron Constantin has recently introduced a number of new models, including the sporty Overseas and the dressy Les Historiques lines, modeled on classic designs from the mid-twentieth century. However, Vacheron Constantin has yet to create an iconic line like Jaeger-LeCoultre's Reverso or Audemars Piguet's Royal Oak. The company has been most successful with its complicated watches, some of which are among the fanciest, yet most reliable, made. And Vacheron Constantin's high-end watches are considered some of the best in the business, produced with tremendous craftsmanship and care. Today few brands can rival the prestige of a Vacheron Constantin timepiece.

Vacheron is known for its cloisonné and enamel work, as exhibited in the distinctive Mercator watch, right. The Mercator series is known for its unusual display of the time. The dial has retrograde sectors graduated for twelve hours and sixty minutes respectively.

FAR LEFT: **VACHERON CONSTANTIN TOLEDO 1952**, 2000s, yellow gold, self-winding mechanical movement with triple-date calendar and moon-phase indicator

LEFT: **VACHERON CONSTANTIN MERCATOR ROYAL EAGLE CHRONOMETER**, 2000s, yellow gold, self-winding mechanical movement with day and date

ABOVE: **VACHERON CONSTAN-TIN MERCATOR REF. 43050**, 1990s, yellow gold with yellow gold dial representing the continents of Europe, Africa, Australia, and Asia, self-winding mechanical movement

RIGHT: **VACHERON CONSTAN-TIN MERCATOR REF. 43050**, 1998, yellow gold with polychrome cloisonné enamel dial representing the Chinese zodiac, self-winding mechanical movement

LEFT: **VACHERON CONSTANTIN CORNES DE VACHE REF. 6087**, 1957, pink gold, mechanical movement with chronograph

RIGHT: **VACHERON CONSTANTIN**, 1930, white and yellow gold, mechanical movement

FAR RIGHT: **VACHERON CONSTANTIN PRESTIGE DE LA FRANCE REF. 2091**, 1972, white gold, mechanical movement

Vacheron Constantin vintage pieces are arguably the equal of Patek Philippe in terms of quality, and although they could once be found for remarkably less, their prices at auction have begun to rise steeply.

BELOW: **VACHERON CONSTANTIN HORIZONTAL SHUTTERS**, 1930, white and yellow gold, mechanical movement

LEFT: **VACHERON CONSTANTIN GEORGE V ROYAL PRESENTATION AVIATOR'S CHRONOGRAPH**, mechanical movement with chronograph. This watch was presented to Admiral Richard Byrd in commemoration of his 1926 Arctic Expedition.

**VACHERON CONSTAN-
TIN CHRONOSCOPE REF.
43040**, 1990s, yellow gold, self-
winding mechanical movement

FAR RIGHT: **VACHERON
CONSTANTIN SALTARELLO
REF. NO. 43041/000R**, 1990s,
pink gold, self-winding
mechanical movement

FROM LEFT TO RIGHT:
**GENÈVE MALTE DUAL TIME
RÉGULATEUR CHRONOMÈTRE
REF. 42005**, 2000, pink gold,
self-winding mechanical
movement with date amd two
time zones

**VACHERON CONSTANTIN
REF. 30020**, late 1990s, yellow
gold, mechanical movement
with perpetual calendar,
minute repeater, and moon-
phase indicator

**VACHERON CONSTANTIN
MALTE REF. 42005**, c. 2000,
white gold, self-winding
mechanical movement
with date

ABOVE: **VACHERON CONSTANTIN**, c. 2000, yellow gold, self-winding mechanical movement with perpetual calendar and moon-phase indicator

RIGHT: **VACHERON CONSTANTIN TOURBILLON MALTE SQUELETTE REF. 30066-67/1**, c. 2000, pink gold, mechanical movement with tourbillon, date, and power-reserve indicator

Among its many strengths, Vacheron Constantin is a master at skeletonization, with unparalleled crafts-manship and delicately filigreed movements for all manner of high complications.

Vacheron Constantin has a legitimate claim to being the oldest high-horology brand. For the company's 250th anniversary in 2005, Vacheron released an in-house automatic movement and a piece that vies for the title of the world's most complicated serially produced wristwatch, the double-sided Tour de l'Lle.

VACHERON CONSTANTIN TOUR DE I'LLE (front and back), 2005, pink gold, mechanical movement with tourbillon, perpetual calendar, minute repeater, second time zone, phases and age of the moon, Sirius star chart, celestial annual calendar, equation of time, as well as power-reserve, day/night, and sunrise/sunset indicators.

Ventura

Ventura is a small Swiss company formed in 1987. Founder Pierre Nobs was flying over the West Coast of the United States; he saw the name Ventura on a map and decided it was well suited to a contemporary watch company.

Unlike many other brands, Ventura's watches aren't modeled on historical archtypes but are instead starkly modern. And instead of relying on gold and platinum, Ventura cases and bracelets are generally constructed of Titanox, which is hardened, scratch-resistant titanium, or of Durinox, an extremely tough variety of steel.

Ventura's designs are atypical and often feature digital displays; the company has the distinction of developing the world's first automatic digital watch that doesn't need a battery (the SPARC fx and px). Perhaps its most famous watch was created by Danish designer Flemming Bo Hansen, who fashioned an LCD watch with an unusually large readout that lies completely flat on a level surface. Not surprisingly it is known as the Flat watch.

The company has also collaborated with design and architecture innovators such as Hannes Wettstein and typographers such as Adrian Frutiger to invent designs that have won many prizes. Ventura watches are displayed in eight museums.

VENTURA V-MATIC MYEGO, 2000s, stainless steel, mechanical movement

VENTURA V-MATIC EGO SQUARE, 2000s, Durinox, self-winding mechanical movement with date

VENTURA V-MATIC EGO FRUTIGER, 2000s, yellow gold, mechanical movement

VENTURA V-MATIC EGO π, 2000s, Titanox, self-winding mechanical movement with date

RIGHT: **VENTURA V-MATIC CHRONO**, 2000s, Titanox, self-winding mechanical movement with chronograph and date

VENTURA V-TEC ALPHA,
2000s, Durinox, electronic
movement with chronograph
and date

VENTURA SPARC FX, 2000s,
Titanox, self-winding quartz
movement with date

VENTURA V-TEC ∑, 2006, Durinox, electronic movement with
chronograph and date

Zenith

Zenith is one of the great manufacturers. The company's watches, which range from moderately priced to high end, are equipped with movements and parts created by Zenith itself; for many years the company also supplied movements to other well-known brands.

The brand was founded in 1865 by Georges Favre-Jacot, and was almost immediately successful, winning many awards, especially for its large movement dubbed the Zenith; this name was eventually adopted as the company's own.

Since 1903, Zenith has been awarded more than fifteen hundred top observatory prizes and medals in chronometry, placing it among the brands with the most awards for precision and reliability.

Zenith was unknown in the United States for many years because it was unable to sell its watches here due to a trademark dispute with the American Zenith Radio Corporation. A resolution seemed imminent when the latter bought the former from the Movado group in the 1970s. The deal didn't turn out well; Zenith watches had lost much of their luster, and by 1983 the company had a new owner, Paul Castella, who reinvigorated the brand before selling it to the LVMH group in 1999.

Today's model line is extensive, but Zenith is still best known for its El Primero chronograph movement, considered by some to be one of the best ever produced; after fifty years, it is still being used to power the company's line of Chrono-Masters (some with multiple complications) as well as its Grande Class El Primero lines.

Also highly successful are the watches in the Elite line, including the Grande Class Elite Power Reserve Dual Time; many watchmakers feel that the Elite movement is actually a better piece of watchmaking than the El Primero, although the latter gets most of the attention.

While it is well-known in Europe, Zenith is making a play to become a leading watch brand in the United States.

ZENITH, c. 1950, stainless steel, mechanical movement

ZENITH EL PRIMERO, 1970s, stainless steel, self-winding mechanical movement with chronograph and date

ZENITH CHRONOMASTER EL PRIMERO movement

ZENITH CHRONOMASTER EL PRIMERO, c. 2000, stainless steel, self-winding mechanical movement with chronograph, date, and moon-phase indicator

LEFT: **ZENITH GRANDE CHRONOMASTER XXT TOURBILLON EL PRIMERO**, 2004, pink gold, self-winding mechanical movement with tourbillon and date

ABOVE: **ZENITH**, 1990s, stainless steel, self-winding mechanical movement

RIGHT: **ZENITH GRANDE CLASS ELITE RÉSERVE DE MARCHE DUAL TIME**, 2000s, rose gold, self-winding mechanical movement with date, two time zones, and power-reserve indicator

OPPOSITE: **ZENITH CHRONOMASTER OPEN EL PRIMERO**, 2005, stainless steel, self-winding mechanical movement with chronograph and power-reserve indicator

It's not actually a brand, but the AHCI (Académie Horlogère des Créateurs Indépendents), deserves mention. Founded in 1984 by watchmakers Svend Andersen and Vincent Calabrese, the academy is composed of many of the best and brightest watchmakers in the business, including Bernhard Lederer, Franck Muller, Christiaan van der Klaauw, François-Paul Journe, George Daniels, Paul Gerber, Philippe Dufour, and Rainer Nienaber.

These watchmakers are, for the most part, the talent behind the scenes at the major companies, although many of them, including Van der Klaauw, Vianney Halter, and Andersen himself, have also created their own eponymous brands. Lederer makes watches under the brand name Blu; others, such as Dufour, Gerber, Roger Smith, Andreas Strehler, Beat Haldimann, and Thomas Prescher, will manufacture custom watches for a considerable price. The prize is a unique timepiece crafted by an expert — something that you alone own.

PHILIPPE DUFOUR
SIMPLICITY, 2000s, platinum, mechanical movement

SVEND ANDERSEN NAVIGA-TION PLEASURE (unique piece), 2005, white gold with marquetry dial, mechanical movement

VIANNEY HALTER CLASSIC,
2000s, rose gold, mechanical
movement

**VINCENT CALABRESE TRANS-
WORLD,** 2000s, platinum,
mechanical movement with
date, two time zones, and
power-reserve indicator

**CHRISTIAAN VAN DER
KLAAUW SATELLITE DU
MONDE** (prototype), 2000s,
stainless steel, self-winding
mechanical movement with
world time and sun indicator

THOMAS PRESCHER TRIPLE AXIS TOURBILLON WITH REMONTOIRE (front and back), 2006, platinum, mechanical movement with tourbillon

BEAT HALDIMANN H1 FLYING CENTRAL TOURBIL-LON THEPURISTS EDITION, 2005, platinum, mechanical movement with tourbillon

AHCI

BUYING, COLLECTING, MAINTAINING

In the opening to his novel *Anna Karenina*, Tolstoy famously remarked that all happy families are alike. Nearly all new watch lovers are alike, too, when they start collecting. Here's what they have in common: They make mistakes.

It's almost impossible not to slip up when you start off — even the most sophisticated connoisseurs will tell you how they overpaid wildly when making their first purchase, or how their first expensive watch lost fifteen minutes a day, or how that wonderful piece that looked so beautiful online turned out to be an ugly mess when it arrived in the mail.

Knowing how to buy watches intelligently takes time, but luckily, mistakes ultimately can be the best teacher.

One watch lover says that when he began his collection he felt Baume & Mercier was the only brand that spoke to him; soon he owned several. Then he decided he preferred Omega and sold his Baume & Merciers at a large loss (having discovered he'd overpaid for them in the first place). He then bought Omegas. That love faded; he moved to Jaeger-LeCoultre, and sold the Omegas — at another loss. And now he has many JLCs, but has found other brands. He realizes that just because he falls in love with a brand today doesn't mean he'll still love it tomorrow.

Another watch lover tells how he started his collection slowly, but when he saw a beautiful Audemars Piguet at a jewelry store, he traded all his old watches for it, not realizing that the old watches were worth far more than the new Audemars Piguets. In effect, he paid twice the store's price, because he didn't understand that the dealer who traded for his watches was simply trying to make as much money as possible.

A third watch aficionado explains how his first purchase was a beautiful 1950s Vacheron Constantin, but the dial was a little soiled, so he had it refinished. He then learned that the watch was worth a great deal more money with the slightly spotty original dial than with its new, cleaned-up face. No one told him that the vintage market places a premium on original condition. The worst part was that the watch looked better with the spotty dial.

Once watch lovers begin to accumulate not just watches but knowledge, they diverge into many camps. No longer alike, aficionados go various ways — some stick to one and only one brand, while others prefer one complication. Some buy to their heart's content; others are restrained by budget considerations. Some care only about the movement, others are interested in the dial. All in all, millions of watches are produced every year, and lying in wait for those watches are millions of different kinds of buyers.

But just as there is one thing almost all watch fans do when they start off — make mistakes — there is something else that everyone who's interested in watches should do for the rest of their watch-collecting careers: Buy intelligently.

You must keep this in mind: The watch business is exactly that — a business. Yes, the industry makes beautiful (continued on page 229)

12 GREAT DRESS WATCHES

I. Patek Philippe Calatrava (Ref. #5196)   2. Breguet Regulateur Automatique

3. Jaeger-LeCoultre Reverso Grand Taille   4. A. Lange & Söhne Lange 1

5. Vacheron Constantin Patrimony 40 Millimeter   6. IWC Portuguese 500107

7. Nomos Tangente   8. Rolex Cellini Prince (2006 Model)

9. Blancpain Villeret Ultraflat   IO. Chopard L.U.C. 1.96

II. Glashütte Panomaticdate   I2. Maurice Lacroix Calendrier Rétrograde

Janklow's Patek, the first Patek wristwatch, 1910

Patek Philippe Caliber 240 movement photographed by Odets

Mort Janklow
Book Agent, New York City

My watch collection started one day as I was walking past a store that sold vintage watches. In the window I saw a perfectly glorious late-1940s Audemars Piguet with the famous neuf millimeters movement, that ultrathin movement that's still the thinnest manual watch ever made.

I thought, that's a beautiful watch, and asked about the price. At the time it seemed expensive: $1,700. I didn't buy it. But I told my wife what I'd seen, and the next thing I knew she bought it for my birthday.

That was just the start. Next I bought an Audemars Quantieme Perpetual. Then many others; soon enough I was thinking and learning about watches regularly. I developed a focus on four favorites: Patek, Audemars, Vacheron, and Rolex. Before I realized it, I was a collector.

My best piece is the very first wristwatch ever made by Patek, which they have certified as such — it dates back to 1910. Patek owned it until 1922, when they sold it; I bought it through a dealer from a descendent of the family. It's one of the most beautiful watches I've ever seen. And I often wear it. In fact, I wear all my watches. I never wear the same one two days in a row, and often switch at nighttime.

With paintings, I am a very careful collector. But I never think about what my next watch might be. It's always serendipitous. That's part of the pleasure.

Walt Odets
Psychotherapist, Berkeley, California

When I started collecting, I knew little about watches. But my father and grandfather had been interested. Here's something my grandfather said that I never forgot: "Patek, Audemars, and Vacheron are great brands, but Jaeger-LeCoultre makes all their watches for them."

As my interest grew, I met a French watchmaker in San Francisco who taught me a great deal about movements. And, since the watch-service business was in disarray, I realized I'd have to learn that part of the watch myself.

Over the years I have owned hundreds and hundreds of watches. But I've cut back on my collection because of the service issue — I don't like to have watches that aren't running properly. At the moment, I have three Pateks, a Blancpain yellow gold split-seconds chronograph, a beautiful 1928 Hamilton Rutledge platinum Tank, and the last of my grandfather's JLCs.

Unlike many collectors, I care about the watch's movement. It's about the craft of design as well as the craft of execution.

I learn much more about a watch by looking at the movement than the dial. You look inside, and you know exactly what the company is about and what they are doing.

Thomas Mao
Corporate Consultant, California

I've been interested in watches since I was six. At first I liked the mechanics; later I developed an eye for the aesthetic, as well as the consumer-psychology aspect of prestige brands.

Growing up, I always felt that most people only dreamed of high-end watches. Most people never get to see, touch, or hear them — either the watches are museum pieces, locked behind glass, or the collectors who own them — like the pieces themselves — are the stuff of legend, existing in some other reality than our own. I've always wanted to create a museum where ordinary people could touch, hear, and feel them; for instance, can you really ever describe the feel of a pusher in words? No, you have to touch it. The same is true for listening to a repeater. You have to hear it in person.

All in all, over the years I've probably gone through more than a thousand pieces. I do have favorites; for some time now it's been an Audemars Piguet Royal Oak with a skeletonized 2120 movement, on top of which there's an engraving of one of the British Royal Oak battleships. It really shouldn't be my favorite; anyone who knows my collection wonders why it's number one. A lot of people think the watch you love should be the one that perfectly epitomizes everything you are pursuing in this particular field. So your favorite watch should be the perfect watch. This AP is gold, and on a gold bracelet; I usually find a gold bracelet too gaudy. And the fact that the watch is skeletonized makes the watch hard to read. But your favorite watch is actually the one you love despite its imperfections. This watch isn't perfect, but I love it the most.

Jeffrey Kingston
Lawyer, East Bay, California

My interest in watches developed by accident while on vacation in Hong Kong. At the time I owned a perfectly fine Rolex Daytona and hadn't devoted a moment's thought to watches. But that day I bought a fabulous Blancpain moon-phase watch. Soon I was fascinated by other complications including chronographs, perpetual calendars, and dual time zones. And because I loved my new watch, I went to the Internet and came across a site called TimeZone. At first I was intimidated by the intelligent dialogue; I was a great lurker before finally stepping forward.

Meanwhile, I bought another Blancpain, a Breguet, a Lange, and so on. Today I have many more watches, but I still love that first Blancpain — it's a fabulous and underappreciated brand.

As my knowledge increases, I'm constantly fascinated by new watches which — keeping the budget at reasonable levels — means having to sell old ones. Perhaps it's a case of discovering that what you truly like evolves over time. You get smarter as you do it. Some watches you might have liked in the early stages of collecting don't seem so special later; for example, I fell for chronographs early on. But it was only with time that I learned the difference between column-wheel and non-column-wheel chronographs; when I did, I decided that only column-wheel chronographs interested me. I want it done the right and traditional way; it's like the difference between instant and real mashed potatoes — I don't want to go to a great restaurant and find that someone microwaved the food. So all the non-column-wheel chronographs I'd purchased had to go.

10 MODELS WHOSE NAMES YOU SHOULD KNOW

1. Royal Oak (Audemars Piguet) 2. Portuguese (IWC) 3. Reverso (Jaeger-LeCoultre)

4. Speedmaster (Omega) 5. Calatrava (Patek Philippe)

6. Monaco (Tag Heuer) 7. Tri-compax (Universal Genève) 8. Santos (Cartier)

9. Museum Watch (Movado) 10. Oyster (Rolex)

pieces of art. But they create these pieces to make a profit. Without profits there can be no craftsmanship, no movement, no dial, no watch.

Look back at the 1970s, when the quartz revolution nearly drove the mechanical watch industry out of business. Hundreds of good companies disappeared forever. The survivors, and the new companies that arose to take advantage of the resurgent love for mechanical watches, learned a lesson. Without the ability to make money from whatever they do, they cease to exist.

The same is true for retailers. A retail store is also a business. Watch sellers with integrity and knowledge exist; it's quite possible to find someone who combines business acumen with integrity. But there are also many retailers for whom getting as much money as possible for a watch is their only consideration.

All that said, accumulating and maintaining a watch collection can be a source of great pleasure. Buying a new watch, or selling an old watch, can feel as emotional as making a new friend, or losing an old one. Many watch collectors keep photographs of all their watches and pass them around the way others might pass around pictures of their children. Some will speak mournfully of a great watch they sold some years before, and what a mistake it was, and how much they miss it. Others will talk about a new watch they just bought and the enormous joy it has brought to their lives.

(And yes, there are others for whom the emotional highs and lows aren't quite as intense. But collecting watches, like any other hobby, often leads to memorable moments.)

Before you start building a collection, take a deep breath. Don't commit to any watch until you're truly ready. It's normal to want to buy everything you see, the moment you see it. In the beginning, many watches will seem interesting and unusual — but they may not be; for example, you may think a complication you've never seen before, such as jumping hours, is completely novel, only to discover that many watch brands make a jump-hour watch (and some do it far better than others). Or you may find your first fly-back chronograph and want to buy it before realizing that it's a fairly common complication and you may have purchased an inferior model.

Be patient. Very few people are so sophisticated that they can move from window-shopper to buyer in one step. Auctions are for the well-versed. The Internet can trip up even the most knowledgeable collectors. Retail stores are filled with pitfalls. Rather than making unnecessary mistakes, do some homework. Here's how:

ACQUIRE A LIBRARY: Find a few books that include information about the watches you like. If you don't want to buy the books, visit a watch store and ask if they'll let you read whatever information they have. Most will be happy to share their resources.

WRITE TO THE MANUFACTURERS TO GET THEIR CATALOGS: Nearly all watch companies will send you a brochure with information about their watches.

GO ONLINE: Web-sites such as TimeZone.com, ThePuristS.com, and EquationofTime.com allow you to read what others have said about the watch you want. Maybe someone else bought it and discovered an inherent flaw; maybe someone else found a way to purchase it for a low price.

TALK TO FELLOW WATCH LOVERS: Ask people who know more than you if your new love is a good buy. Find out if the watch is historically important, if the dial is original, if the movement is good, and so on.

VISIT WATCH STORES: Not all retail outlets are good places to make a purchase; while some are honest and aboveboard, others can be risky. But you can still look at the watches, try them on, and see how they fit. Make a connection with a well-informed salesperson. These people often know a great deal about the industry, such as when a watch might go on sale, when the model line is going to be discontinued, and so on. (But don't become overly concerned with other opinions. The final test of a watch is whether or not you like it and want to wear it. Sometimes you will love a watch that no one else appreciates. There's nothing wrong with that.)

If you're not patient, you may end up in this common trap: You see a watch, you want it, you buy it. A month later, you hate it. Nearly every watch collector has fallen in love at first sight only to fall out of love soon afterward. Watches can be like people; the first impression is excellent, the next isn't.

Here's a tip from a collector who's been burned often: Whenever he sees a new watch he likes, he clips its photo on his refrigerator. His policy: If, after looking at it every day for a month, he finds no other watch he likes more, he's confident the watch will have lasting power.

If you don't have a photo, go online where you can find an image of nearly every watch ever made. Paste the image into a file of prospective purchases, and look at it often before buying.

Another tip: If you have an urge simply to make a purchase, think about buying something small to satisfy your craving. A fresh band can make an old watch look new again, and you'll have spent a fraction of the money.

And before you buy, think about what you actually want to wear. Some serious watch collectors buy a timepiece and place it in a safe. Is this what you really want? Sometimes the right watch isn't the one that looks best in the vault, but on your wrist.

You may like your watch better, and for a longer time, if it suits your personality; for example, if you're an informal person, a fragile gold vintage piece may end up in your drawer forever. And if you're the kind who prefers graceful, slim watches, why buy a big multi-complication sports watch, even if it's a bargain? Likewise, if you've never traveled more than a few hundred miles from your hometown, is a dual-time-zone item really right for you?

Still, nearly everyone makes mistakes. Bad purchases happen. Don't let them spoil your enthusiasm. Your mistakes are learning experiences; if you bought a fake, you now know how to avoid the next. If you bought a watch you don't like, you now have a better understanding of your taste.

One way to avoid mistakes is to focus on a particular kind of watch. The world of timepieces is enormous. There are hundreds of brands, dozens of complications, millions of vintage watches for sale. You may find that by choosing one area to study, you'll profit from limiting the seemingly infinite. You might want to start off with just American brands, such as vintage Hamiltons or Gruens. Or you may want to look into duo-dial watches. Or, pick a quality Swiss brand, such as Fortis or Oris, that appeals to you but isn't as expensive as the top-end brands.

One simple way to avoid mistakes: Put the watch on your wrist before you buy it. A watch that looks excellent in a photo may look terrible on you. A watch is like any other accessory — even the best-looking one may not flatter you. Some people have rounded wrists, making flat watches look silly; others have thin wrists and oversized watches hang over the edge.

Here are additional areas to think about:

BRANDS: There is no real top ten; it's all relative. Each brand has strengths and weaknesses. If you like a particular brand, learn as much as you can about it. But be ready for someone who will tell you it's not as good as Brand X. For him, it isn't; for you, it may be perfect.

COMPLICATIONS: Not everyone likes them, but they can add value to a watch. Although some time-only watches are worth a great deal of money, generally the most sought-after watches feature a complication such as a chronograph, a perpetual calendar, a repeater, or a combination of many. But bear in mind that complicated watches can be delicate, and service costs run high. It's a rude awakening to discover that although you could sell your tourbillon for $5,000 over its original price, it costs more than that to service it. And, since very complicated watches are often fragile, you probably won't want to wear them every day.

TRENDS: Be wary of them. For example, it seems as if watches grow larger each year. Will this trend last? No one knows. If you're concerned with long-term value, be careful. If you like a large watch regardless of fashion, follow your heart. But if you're thinking about the future, remember that tastes change: The ultra-large watch that's so hip today could be tomorrow's extra-wide lapels.

(*continued on page 233*)

9 WATCH BRANDS THAT ARE LESS EXPENSIVE THAN THEY LOOK

1. ORIS   2. LIMES   3. LONGINES   4. NOMOS   5. TISSOT (especially the replica Chronos)

6. RADO   7. DAVOSA   8. EPOS   9. STOWA

Friedberg's IWC Mark X

Gurevitz's JLC Military WWW

Michael Friedberg
Lawyer, Chicago, Illinois

I first became interested in watches in around 1987 when I bought a Rolex GMT 2. I'm not sure why I bought it — maybe because it looked great and everyone said it was the world's best watch. Then in 1990, while traveling in Ireland, I saw an Omega watch with a complicated calendar. Soon I'd traded my Rolex.

At one point I was up to fifty watches, but I've cut back to far fewer. All but three are IWCs; the others are a Rolex, a Patek 3940 perpetual calendar, and a special limited-edition Panerai.

My favorite watch is the one I bought yesterday. It's easy to fall in love with your last date. But IWC is my brand. In fact, I'm proud to be the professional moderator of its online forum.

For me, a mechanical watch is an object of industrial art — a synthesis of both design and mechanics. But it's hard to articulate why something has a great design. It's so subjective. It's not like watching a movement in a vibrograph; so many underlying design principles are extremely important. And then there's good mechanics, which watch people love to discuss and which I think can be vastly overrated. Essentially all watches keep time. Some do it better than others, but the parameters are often meaningless in the real world. Unless you're OCD, you're really talking about artistry.

The world of watch collectors is fascinating. I have a Freudian theory about people who get so angry or so defensive about their collection — their sense of self and self-esteem become so quickly activated; I don't know why. Maybe because a watch can be a symbol; it's a primarily masculine object, which is why large watches sell so well. You can talk about utility of watches, and how large watches are easier to read, but to a lot of people they may simply be a form of reassurance.

Frankly, I think the psychology of the watch collector is a more interesting subject than watches themselves.

Steve Gurevitz
Private Investor, Ohio

Way back when I worked in a warehouse, I wore a plain Rado, which I liked — so much, in fact, that I got my wife a smaller version. But her battery kept dying every year, so I started wondering if there were watches that didn't need them, and I ended up buying her a Citizen automatic (which I paid too much for).

I then decided I should have a watch like that too and consulted the Web. I didn't know mechanical watches even existed. Soon I became hooked. I bought a Minerva. An Audemars Piguet dress watch (my first and last eBay purchase). An Audemars perpetual (for which I paid too much, again).

At that point I thought I'd have two or three watches, one for every occasion. But then two things happened: One was finding a Peseux 260 watch, and becoming very interested in these 1940s and 1950s movements. The other was my new camera. When I started taking pictures of watches, I really began seeing them for the first time.

So I bought more, and more — a Roger Dubuis, a Journe Octa, a Grand Seiko. Today I have about seventy watches. But I don't think of myself as a collector. I'm an accumulator. The difference is that a collector has a theme, a central focus, a strong purpose that is perhaps higher than "I buy what I like."

My only theme is: If I don't wear it, I don't keep it. I am not trying to preserve them for the future as a collector should. I just like them.

I can't say I have a favorite but at the moment I'm very fond of World War II military watches — especially the Jaeger-LeCoultres. There are twelve official World War II watches. The famous ones are Omega and IWC, but I like the JLCs, because the company made fabulous movements. Everyone else took their best twenty-eight-millimeter movement and adopted it for the watch, but JLC designed a new one.

The back of Jordão's F. P. Journe
Resonance

The dial of Boutros's
Rolex COMEX Submariner

Felipe Jordão
Financial Analyst, New York City

When I was a baby, I'd always start crying at the exact moment I was supposed to be fed. So my mother called me her little Patek (which made me Patek Felipe.) Maybe that made an impression.

Later, growing up, whenever my parents took me past a watch shop, I'd stick my face right on the window and stare. Not that I understood the mechanical aspects of watches — I just thought they were cool.

But I couldn't afford to buy them yet, although in college I did buy a lot of Swatches.

Then, about six years ago, I got a TAG for Christmas — my first really nice watch. A few years later I started taking watches seriously, and soon was going online to watch sites and looking around. After deciding my next watch should be a Jaeger-LeCoultre, I started researching, and eventually bought a Reverso Duo. Then I bought a Reverso Sun/Moon in rose gold. Now I really had the bug. I started thinking of all these other categories of watches I desperately needed to have. I got a Zenith El Primero. I got a Minerva pilot's watch. I saved up and got a Lange Up and Down in platinum. Then the Lange 1815 in yellow gold. From there I started selling some pieces, buying others. I decided I had to have an F. P. Journe Octa with a moon phase and traded the 1815 plus some cash for it.

Once I had the Journe, all bets were off. Deep down I always wanted another Journe — the Resonance. So I started scheming on how to get it; I now own one.

And about a year and a half ago, I ordered the watch I most wanted — a custom-made piece by English watchmaker Roger Smith; it comes with the English finishing and frosted gilt finish like the old watches. And it has the coaxial escapement, which Smith learned from the inventor, George Daniels. If everything goes well it should be ready within the next twelve months. The anticipation makes it all the more exciting.

Paul Boutros
Electrical Engineer, New Jersey

My interest in watches began when I was ten. My father and I walked into a watch boutique and saw a $23,000 IWC pocket watch; the moment I saw its movement, it was love at first sight, the beginning of a lifelong passion, and also an important bond between my father and me — my relationship with my father was tempestuous at times, but we both loved watch collecting.

When my father died, I inherited a collection of one hundred and fifty watches we'd bought together, including several Patek Philippe, Rolex, and Omega wristwatches. I consider myself the steward of that collection.

When buying, I follow my heart. I buy what I love: vintage Rolex sports watches, Vacheron Constantins, Patek Philippes, and Omegas. As an engineer, I appreciate these brands' devotion to precision and excellence.

Among my Rolex pieces, I've been very fortunate to acquire several rare models, including a prototype Sea Dweller, one of twelve known; a rare British Navy–issued military Submariner, one of fewer than one hundred known; and a special COMEX Submariner, one of 156 made. But the watch I'm most proud of is among the rarest of all Rolexes — it's known as the Kew A — and contains a movement, one of 144, handmade and regulated by Jean Matile, Rolex's top watchmaker during the mid-1900s. One hundred twenty were cased in boy's-sized steel cases and sold in 1949. In 1954, twenty-four were cased in men's-sized 18-karat-gold cases. Mine is the latter type, and is one of three known to exist in original condition. They are probably the most precise wristwatches ever sold to the public by any brand.

Watches are the synthesis of much of what I most love: science, history, art, design, culture, and craftsmanship. And collecting them helps keep the spirit of my father alive; it's a constant reminder of the wonderful times we shared together.

RARITY: In general, the rarer the watch, the more likely it is to hold its value. Sometimes this is obvious: A Patek Philippe limited edition means exactly that — few other people will have the watch and that gives it a premium. But there are thousands of limited editions on the market, and just because only a few of each type of watch were made doesn't necessarily mean they're going to become valuable.

MATERIAL: Metal matters. Gold-filled watches generally tend to be worth less than watches made of gold itself. Platinum is generally worth more; if you're browsing a flea market and find an old platinum Hamilton, assuming the watch is in good shape, you may have hit the jackpot. However, a more expensive metal doesn't always mean a more expensive watch. A. Lange & Söhne made only a handful of stainless steel Lange 1s, and therefore a steel Lange 1 is more valuable today than a gold one.

MOVEMENTS: When you're buying a watch, consider learning about its insides. You don't need to be an expert on movements; few people are. But a good salesperson should be willing to let you look inside the watch, especially if it is a vintage edition. (This does not hold true for many modern watches, where you may void a warranty if you open the case.) (For more on movements see page 240.)

FAKES: The fake watch industry has boomed in recent years. Be vigilant. Some fakes are well done, but many are obvious. Look at the dial and the case back. Are all the words spelled correctly? Is the case appropriate for the model? Is the lettering consistent with the brand? People often take good movements and place them in new cases because the old ones were damaged. A smart watchmaker can point this out for you. He can also show you how to discriminate between an average fake and a sophisticated one, in which original parts from different watches have been used to make one seemingly authentic piece.

CONDITION: The state of the watch is important. And this doesn't refer just to a watch looking battered or beaten. Most novices don't take into account what's known as a refinished dial. Dials are the face of the watch, and just as people refinish their own faces through plastic surgery, dials that become overly scratched or oxidized are often refinished in such a way as to make them look like they are original. The problem: In the world of collecting, original condition is important. So even though it might seem counter-intuitive, a watch with an original, somewhat damaged dial is generally worth more than the same watch with a beautiful new dial.

Sometimes a redial is easy to detect; the new lettering is slightly askew, or the numbers aren't quite in the right place. At other times, it takes an expert's inspection to identify.

Likewise, if a watch has been heavily polished, it won't be worth as much. Again, original condition is an important part of collecting.

PAPERS: Whenever you buy a vintage watch, risk is involved. Check to see if the original box and particularly the paperwork are available. If so, that may add as much as 25 percent more value to the watch.

When you've decided what watch to buy, be suspicious if you're being offered a surprising deal. Whenever someone wants to save you money, try to understand why. Bargains exist, but they're rare.

Also, is price what really matters? If you find a watch you truly love and it's a hundred dollars more than you wanted to spend, does that mean you shouldn't buy it? Some of your most beloved watches won't be bargains, but they'll be lifetime investments.

Some people feel that the seller is as important a consideration as the watch itself. Finding a seller you can trust is crucial. If you buy from a reputable source, you are much more likely to be getting what you want.

When buying, remember that the sticker price isn't always the real price. You may not be able to bargain at a standard department store, but at most outlets, haggle. No one buys a car at the sticker price; the same holds true for most watches. Yes, a few salespeople may look at you like you're crazy, but even there, you won't be the first person who's tried.

Auctions are an excellent source of vintage — and sometimes new — watches, giving you the opportunity to buy a great watch at a discount price. But before you bid, go

12 NEW BRANDS TO LOOK OUT FOR

I. ANGULAR MOMENTUM   2. ANONIMO   3. D.FREEMONT   4. FRÉDÉRIQUE CONSTANT   5. JACQUES ETOILE

6. MEISTERSINGER   7. NIVREL   8. AUGUSTE REYMOND   9. RGM   10. SOTHIS   11. TEMPTION   12. XEMEX

to the exhibition and look at the piece. If you don't go to the preview, you won't be prepared to make an appropriate offer. Antiquorum, for example, offers condition reports in its catalog, but other auction houses may expect you to ask for them.

Maintaining Watches

Once you've bought your watch, only you can keep it in good shape. A watch is a small, finely tuned instrument. While a good one can last many generations, any mechanical device — and certainly one so tiny — will need caring attention to guarantee that it functions at the peak of its capacity. This means that if you're going to collect watches, you'll have to take good care of them.

Unfortunately, the watch-repair business is itself in need of repair. One of the best watch technicians, Manhattan-based Alkis Kotsopoulos, says that the primary problem he deals with is the incompetent work done by other watch repairers. He tells the story of a client who'd just purchased a beautiful vintage Rolex chronograph. But when Kotsopoulos opened it, he discovered that so many others had worked on the watch that the movement was in terrible shape: screws had been replaced and now barely fit, the balance wheel was bent, and the hairspring was unrepairable. There was nothing Kotsopoulos could do but return the watch to his customer and tell him the truth: The watch might never work.

The number of excellent watch experts seems to be shrinking each year. Finding someone whom you can trust won't be easy, but it can be done. The best way to find an expert is to ask friends or to post a query at one of the better watch forums on the Internet.

Following are some tips to help you keep your watch in good condition.

READ YOUR MANUAL: Many watches come with a manual. Read it carefully, just as you would any other manual for a complicated device. The better you understand your watch, the more likely it is to behave well.

KEEP YOUR WATCHES CLEAN: Before you put your watch away after wearing it all day, wipe off the grime on the back. Don't let the case become a receptacle of dirt.

WIND YOUR WATCHES: At least once a month, wind your watches to give them running time (some people advise as much as once a week, but no one knows the precise answer). You don't need to set them if you're not wearing them, but they will perform best if they get wound now and then.

Many people who own automatic watches use winders, or electrically operated devices that wind automatic watches when the timpiece isn't in use. Watch winders work best for watches with a perpetual calendar (or some other complex astronomical complication) — you won't have to reset the watch every time you wear it.

WIND AND SET CAREFULLY: Place your fingers on both sides of the crown when you wind. If you wind the watch using just one side, you'll be putting pressure in one direction, causing wear on the movement if the stem moves upward. When you use both sides of the crown, you're applying even pressure.

For a plain, manual watch, it doesn't matter whether you set the time by moving the hands backward or forward. But it can make a difference on a complicated watch, and there are a few (such as minute-repeating watches) that will be damaged if you rotate the hands counterclockwise.

KEEP YOUR WATCH DRY: If your watch is not water-resistant, or only mildly so, avoid moisture. Watch repairers such as Kotsopoulos tell of people who complain that their watch inexplicably stopped, only to find that it's simply waterlogged. Many people don't realize that total waterproofing is next to impossible; the best you can hope for is a high degree of water resistance.

(continued on page 236)

Sandler's Patek Philippe
Calatrava #5053

Cramer's Cartier Pasha with its
Figaro bracelet

Michael Sandler
Operations Manager, New Jersey

When I was a kid I took apart anything that was mechanical, especially clocks — much to my father's chagrin. From there my love of watches became an infatuation. I started wearing them when I was four; my first watch was a hand-me-down from my father. Later, I saved my allowance and used the money from my paper route to buy inexpensive digital watches. In my late teens, I became interested in mechanical watchmaking. But I didn't have the money to buy good watches yet; after college, as my earning power grew, so did my collection.

I've probably owned about two hundred watches, although at the moment I have far fewer. I don't like to buy watches that sit in boxes, so if I don't enjoy a watch, I'll sell it. I'm not a safe queen; I don't have the money to keep a $5,000 watch in a vault. I'd rather take that money and buy another.

Although it changes, my favorite brands are Patek, Audemars, Jaeger-LeCoultre, and IWC; my favorite watch is my Patek #5053, the officer's-case Calatrava in rose gold. And if I could buy any new watch, it would be the new Breguet Marine. I love the dial; for me it's not just about the movement but the overall aesthetic.

My preoccupation with watches led me to run the Internet Web-site TimeZone.com; I've been involved with the operations since 1998. I have a more than full-time career, but I can put as much as twenty-five hours a week into the site. I'm also a severe insomniac, so much of what I do on TimeZone takes place after my family's in bed. It's an excellent distraction from the fact that I'm alone in the house for four hours a night before I go to sleep.

George Cramer
Art Director, Nice, France

As a record company art director, I've always been interested in beauty, particularly in industrial design, furniture, and architecture. Everything I buy needs to look good — even if another product is better, I'll choose the one with the best design.

I'm also very attracted to tradition as well as excellent craftsmanship. And, as an album-cover designer, I've been fascinated by the square, as a canvas or just as a design element. There's something about a square that inspires me.

It isn't a coincidence, then, that the brand that combines all my aesthetic interests is Cartier. My first watch was the square Santos; a few years later I traded it for the original Santos Dumont, which is also square.

Staying with Cartier, in 1985 I bought the just-released Pasha watch with a grill on a leather strap. At that time, there was also a stunning Figaro bracelet available for the watch, but it was soon replaced by a newer, but less interesting model. I desperately wanted that original Figaro bracelet, but I didn't have the funds.

Still, I kept watching and waiting, until the bracelet sold out in Europe and I realized that if I didn't act, I'd never be able to buy one. Then I heard from a friend that a boutique in Miami, Florida, still had one in stock. Although I wanted it badly I didn't have the money. So I took a bold step: I sold my car, booked a holiday in Miami, and bought the best watch bracelet Cartier ever made.

11 MODERN WATCHES THAT LOOK VINTAGE

I. Breguet Manual Winding   2. Harwood Automatic

3. Jaquet Droz Grande Seconde Cerclée   4. Maurice Lacroix Pontos Small Seconds

5. A. Lange & Söhne 1815   6. Longines Master Collection Automatic   7. Minerva Pythagore

8. Movado Semi Moon   9. Patek Philippe Calatrava (ref. #5196)

10. Stowa Airman 47040   11. Union Glashütte Johannes Dürrstein 1

Water resistance is only as good as the watch's gaskets. A watch frequently exposed to soap, salt, or a sauna will run a high damage risk.

If you see condensation under the crystal, bring the watch to a watchmaker. Rust on steel parts can form within a day if salt water is collecting inside.

And remember that you should have your watch's water resistance verified once a year, as manufacturers recommend (practically no one actually does).

DON'T JOLT YOUR WATCH: You know better than to drop your watch on the floor. But do you know better than to wear your gold watch next to a bracelet or gold chain? Gold is a soft material, and the friction of one metal against another will scratch the case; a stainless steel or titanium watch resists scratches better.

SERVICE YOUR WATCH: Most watch experts believe a watch should be serviced as often as the manufacturer recommends.

A vocal minority claims that servicing can actually hurt a watch, because the potential for damage is high. One expert says, "A modern piece with readily available parts probably shouldn't be serviced until it stops performing well, makes funny noises, or otherwise misbehaves. The chances of the movement being damaged during regular service by a watchmaker are at least as great as the chances of doing any real damage by just running it until it can't run anymore. And, in general, the cost of watch service will not be any greater even if a major part needs to be replaced (at a manufacturer's service center). Such a course of action for a very expensive, complicated, or rare piece is probably unwise, likewise for a vintage piece without readily available replacement parts, but for a modern Rolex, IWC, or Omega, for example, it is hard to refute."

STORE YOUR WATCHES CAREFULLY: The more airtight, and therefore dust-free, the environment the better — especially for vintage watches. You don't need to find a vacuum, but don't store them in the bathroom or any other place where the humidity could seep inside the case. A flat, dry place is best.

DON'T EXPECT PERFECT TIME: Be patient with a vintage watch. Even a great watch may lose a few minutes a day. An old watch is more fragile than a new one; the shock-resistance systems the watch industry uses today did not appear until the mid-twentieth century. For the most part, vintage watches can be worn every day, but only if you are careful.

IF YOUR WATCH BREAKS, BRING IT BACK TO THE STORE WHERE YOU BOUGHT IT: If this isn't possible, deal directly with the manufacturer. Some of the newer brands may not have an international service program, making it difficult to find a convenient repair operation. So you may have to send the watch to the manufacturer, which generally means to Europe. If you can't do this, find a talented repairer who will try to find original parts before improvising.

Be patient. Watch repair can be a lengthy process. The parts may not be readily available.

DON'T CHANGE THE BATTERY: That is, don't change it yourself. Take the watch to an expert and let him or her do it. Unless you're very knowledgeable, you could damage the watch when you open it and leave behind unsightly scratches. And if your battery-operated watch has stopped, have the batteries changed immediately before the old battery drips fluid onto the movement.

If you're not wearing your battery-operated watch, some feel it is best to remove the battery to extend its life, as well as to reduce wear and tear on the watch. Others claim it is better to let the battery stay inside the watch and die in two years rather than try to save it, because the battery may leak and the resulting acid spillover can destroy a movement.

12 GREAT VINTAGE WATCHES

(Some of these watches are still being made today, but this list refers only to the vintage models.)

1. **PATEK PHILIPPE CALATRAVA (REF. #96):** small by today's standards, but pure design and an icon

2. **PATEK PHILIPPE (REF. #2526):** one of the most beautiful automatics ever made

3. **PATEK PHILIPPE PERPETUAL (REF. #3450):** a very important perpetual calendar, and at least a rare beauty

4. **ROLEX DAYTONA:** the great sports chronograph

5. **ROLEX BUBBLEBACK:** there's no one paradigm model, but the historical significance to this watch can't be underestimated

6. **ROLEX SUBMARINER (REF. #5512):** there are rarer Rolexes, but this may be the most historically important dive watch

7. **IWC MARK XI:** the classic military watch par excellence

8. **JAEGER-LECOULTRE REVERSO:** the 1930s classic, and art deco at its finest

9. **VACHERON CONSTANTIN TRIPLE CALENDAR (REF. #4240):** a stellar example of fine work, fine design, and classic Swiss craftsmanship

10. **BREITLING NAVITIMER:** an important aviator's chronograph, but also a great-looking watch

11. **UNIVERSAL GENÈVE TRI-COMPAX:** from the 1940s and 1950s, a very underrated model; it helped popularize the complicated watch

12. **AUDEMARS PIGUET ULTRA SLIM:** the ultra-slim AP cal 2003 is one of the most elegant watches ever produced, and no one cased the slim movement better than Audemars; the watch is only four-millimeters thick

8 MANUAL-WIND CHRONOGRAPHS

1. **A LANGE & SÖHNE DATOGRAPH:** one of the most finely manufactured traditional chronographs ever made

2. **PATEK PHILIPPE 5070:** perhaps the other best manufactured chronograph

3. **OMEGA SPEEDMASTER:** the watch that went to the moon

4. **JAEGER-LECOULTRE REVERSO SPORT CHRONOGRAPH:** very cool, underappreciated piece

5. **GLASHÜTTE PANOGRAPH:** gorgeous, if slightly quirky design

6. **ULYSSE NARDIN CHRONOGRAPH MONOPUSHER:** with a Jacquet movement, a nice-looking watch

7. **CARTIER CHRONOGRAPH MONOPUSHER:** similar to the Ulysse Nardin in looks, but with the added Cartier cachet

8. **GIRARD-PERREGAUX MONOPUSHER:** also similar to the Ulysse Nardin, but nonetheless a great watch

14 WATCHES THAT ARE FUN TO WATCH

I. Bell & Ross 123 Jumping Hour: everyone should own one jump-hour watch; this is one of the coolest

2. Martin Braun EOS: because you can see when the sun will rise and set, even if you don't care

3. Breitling B-2: perhaps the busiest dial ever made

4. Chronoswiss Pathos: reasonably affordable skeleton chronograph by a reliable brand

5. Eberhard Chrono 4: there are four subdials at the bottom of the dial; no one's done it before

6. Girard-Perregaux Rattrapante with Lightning Seconds: like something out of a carnival, a hand spins around one full rotation per second

7. Graham Chronofighter: the crown is almost as big as the watch

8. Jaquet Droz Grand Seconde Marine: looks more like an eighteenth-century piece than many actual eighteenth-century pieces

9. Jaeger-LeCoultre Gyrotourbillon: watching the aluminum sphere rotate the escapement through two different axes is mesmerizing

10. JeanRichard Tv Screen Seconds Retrograde: the second hand goes back and forth like a windshield wiper

11. Maurice Lacroix Cinq Aieuilles: perhaps one of the best designed of all the busy-faced watches

12. Ulysse Nardin Freak: no hands, all movement

13. Ventura V-Tec Alpha: resembles something from *Star Wars*, with a cool scroll knob to locate its many complications

14. Vianney Halter Antiqua: because it looks like nothing else in the world

9 WATCHES TO MAKE YOU FEEL YOU'RE IN A COCKPIT

I. Breguet Type 21: nice successor to the Type 20 and the vintage Breguets

2. Blancpain Flyback: excellent chronograph movement

3. Hanhart Fliegerchronograph Replica: traditionalist's favorite

4. Tutima Flieger Chronograph 1941: ditto

5. IWC Mark XV Classic: the blueprint of the basic Swiss pilot's watch; indeed, perhaps the basic Swiss mechanical watch

6. Breitling Navitimer: a historical classic

7. Rolex GMT II: versatile, durable, classic, and used by PanAm

8. Laco (a vintage World War II model): few watches look better on a wrist

9. Glycine Airman 5: almost large enough to be an actual cockpit panel clock

Designer Watches

Most of the watches in this book were designed by professionals employed by watch companies, but wristwatches have tempted fashion, graphic, and industrial designers since they became popular at the turn of the last century. So-called designer watches have a way of looking dated over time (and some look dated the moment they're made), but here is a list of companies making some of the best designer watches today. Not surprisingly, many of them use quartz movements, since designers tend to focus on the watch's look rather than its mechanics.

ISSEY MIYAKE. Miyake, Japan's foremost fashion designer, has commissioned four series of unusual watches for his company since 2001. Insetto, designed by Shunji Yamanaka, was inspired by the exoskeletons and antennae of insects. It was later joined by Vakio, designed by Harri Koskinen; To, designed by Tokujin Yoshioka; and Twelve, designed by Naoto Fukasawa. All, with the exception of a few of the Insettos, have quartz movements and are manufactured by SII (Seiko Instruments Inc. Japan). These watches feel fresh and distinctive.

CHANEL. Jacques Helleu, artistic director of Chanel, designed the company's first unisex sports watch, the J12, in 2000, and the line has proliferated. The watch combines a traditional chronograph dial with an innovative ceramic case and automatic Swiss movement.

IKEPOD. Launched in 1994 as a vehicle for designer Mark Newson, Ikepod eventually went out of business, but new watches are still available. These watches strike a balance between Newson's design aesthetic and traditional watchmaking (they are made with good Swiss mechanical movements).

MONDAINE. The official Swiss railway clock designed by Hans Hilfiker in the 1940s was an icon of modernism that spawned a wristwatch in 1986. Since then, this Swiss company has created many variations of that classic design with quartz movements; they are beloved by graphic designers everywhere.

MAX BILL BY JUNGHANS. Junghans, the German company that has pioneered the manufacture of radio-controlled watches, has also produced high-quality mechanical versions of the watches that the Bauhaus designer Max Bill created for the company in the early 1960s.

ALESSI WATCHES. This co-venture of Alessi, an Italian company with a seemingly vast output of modern design objects, and SII (Seiko Instruments Inc. USA), offers an influential line of contemporary designer watches, all of which are quartz. Among its well-known designers are Achille Castiglioni, Aldo Rossi, Ron Arad, Piero Lissoni, and Alberto Meda.

PIERRE JUNOD. This Swiss company manufactures quartz watches designed by prominent designers and architects, including especially interesting contributions by Steven Götz, Arne Jacobsen, Mario Botta, and the Vignellis.

PHILIPPE STARCK AND FRANK GEHRY BY FOSSIL. Fossil, an American company that manufactures inexpensive quartz watches, has commissioned lines from these two very prominent designers. Both feature large digital displays.

BELOW: **IKEPOD MANATEE**, 2003, stainless steel, self-winding mechanical movement with world time

ABOVE: **MONDAINE CLASSIC**, 2005, stainless steel, quartz movement

Movements

Most people have no idea what makes their watches tick — literally. They've never looked inside; the movement is of little to no interest to them. Watchmakers claim it isn't uncommon for a customer to bring in a watch that isn't working well and ask if it needs a new battery. The watch turns out to be automatic, and the only reason the watch isn't working is that the owner hasn't been wearing it.

This isn't to say that to appreciate watches you must know how they work. But there's something to be said for looking inside a watch and beholding the small miracle called a movement. Not only are you peering back into history — the mechanical movement in today's watch is in many ways the same as that found in a clock dating from 1500 — but you are also examining a remarkable piece of machinery. These days, you often don't even have to remove the back of a watch to see its movement. More and more watches come with crystal-covered backs that allow you to gaze inside and behold the inner workings. And if you have a mechanical bent, you can buy a very inexpensive watch and experiment with it. Every time you take a watch apart, you risk sacrificing a little of its excellence as you put it back together — even if you're an expert — but there's great satisfaction to be had in dismanteling and reassembling a watch movement.

To collectors who love movements — and there are legions of them — not knowing about a movement is akin to owning a sports car but being clueless about the engine. Such enthusiasts say the culture of a watch company is readily apparent from a look inside one of its creations.

The beauty lies in craftsmanship — the craft of design, as well as the craft of execution; for instance, some will wax poetic about the beauty of, say, the Patek 240 movement. It's something wonderful, they declare, perhaps the greatest movement around. A simple flat, automatic movement with a minimum number of parts, it manages to make every part count, and every part that counts is elegant and beau-

tifully executed. The Patek 240 epitomizes what makes a movement great.

What else makes a movement great? Visual details. A movement can involve just as many aesthetic choices as the dial. The shape of the parts is not always functionally determined — some of them can be fashioned with straight lines and sharp angles or smooth sweeping curves, purely at the whim of the designer. The finishing makes the movement seem to glow with a patina as distinct as the dial's. (Finishing, the last step in the production of any part or component, generally refers to the decorative detailing of the watch movement or case.)

Interest in watch movements has surged since the Internet created a forum for displaying and viewing photos of watches that could never before have been accessed so easily. Enthusiasts began sharing their observations and opinions of different movements, and asking questions of watch companies. In response, the industry listened and changed. Many experts feel that the level of finishing has improved over the last decade as a result. And few companies dare sell expensive watches with inexpensive movements today. In short, companies can no longer say whatever they want about a product — they know that their movements are being scrutinized by the world.

ABOVE LEFT TO RIGHT:
LANGE L941.1
PHILIPPE DUFOUR SIMPLICITY
JLC 975

LEFT TO RIGHT:
GLASHÜTTE ORIGINAL 95
JLC CAL. 822
AUDEMARS PIGUET 3120

7 GREAT MANUAL MOVEMENTS

1. **AUDEMARS PIGUET 3090**: a gorgeous watch, with a free-sprung balance under a bridge and no corners cut in its manufacture or decoration

2. **VACHERON CONSTANTIN 1400**: slightly more traditional and conventional than the Audemars Piguet 3090, but more beautiful to look at

3. **PATEK PHILIPPE 215**: not the most attractive bridge layout, but perfectly executed; Patek is the king for a reason

4. **JAEGER-LECOULTRE CAL. 822**: the classic Reverso movement; a wonderfully executed old-school design that works well

5. **PHILIPPE DUFOUR SIMPLICITY**: the watchmaker's favorite but hard to find

6. **LANGE L941.1**: excellent overall execution with unparalleled decorative finishing

7. **PIGUET 21**: generally considered the best of the ultrathin movements

8 GREAT AUTOMATIC MOVEMENTS

1. **ROLEX 3135**: perhaps the most accurate, robust, and serviceable automatic on the planet; the only mass-produced automatic with an overcoil hairspring, a significant contributor to good accuracy across positions and states of wind

2. **AUDEMARS PIGUET 3120**: the last few years have seen the high-end players come to their senses as far as accuracy and reliability are concerned; this company is now making its movements thicker and is adopting some battle-tested features such as free-sprung balances, balance bridges, beefier parts, and jeweled calendar mechanisms (the race to make the thinnest movement seems to have ended)

3. **JAEGER-LECOULTRE 975** (as found in the new Compressor Dualmatic and Master Hometime): combines fine watchmaking with ruggedness; features a full bridge, a free-sprung balance with locking stud carrier, and high-tech features such as ceramic ball bearings

4. **ETA 2892**: the best mass-produced movement, available in a wide variety of watches; for an entry-level chronometer-grade automatic, this is a great performer

5. **OMEGA 2500**: offers the new coaxial escapement designed by George Daniels to minimize or even eliminate lubrication, in addition to other modifications by Omega

6. **GIRARD-PERREGAUX 3300**: a highly refined hand-setting train gives very positive hand-setting action too; it is also quite thin

7. **PIGUET 1150**: with two barrels and one hundred hours of power reserve—and pretty to look at

8. **GLASHÜTTE ORIGINAL 95**: the three-quarter sized rotor offers a compromise between small, but often inefficient, microrotors and the rotors that hide most of the movement

HOROLOGY FROM A TO Z

ADJUSTED: The process by which the rate of the watch is aligned to be as close as possible in different physical positions, as well as in different states of winding (for example, fully wound versus after twenty-four hours running) and in different temperatures. A fully adjusted watch is typically one that is adjusted for five positions (crown down, crown left, crown up, dial up, and dial down), isochronism (states of wind), and temperature (both heat and cold), for a total of eight adjustments.

ALARM WATCH: A watch with a built-in bell or buzzer that can be set to ring at a specific time.

AMPLITUDE: The maximum angular displacement of the balance wheel from its resting position, measured in degrees. Often used as an indicator of a watch movement's running health.

ANALOG DISPLAY: There are two kinds of time displays: One is called analog, which is the standard dial formation with hands (generally hour, minute, and second); the other display is called digital, and it displays the time as a readout, i.e., 7:32. The latter is usually displayed through the LED or LCD, although some mechanical watches have digital displays using discs that can be seen through apertures.

ANNUAL CALENDAR: A calendar mechanism that automatically adjusts itself for the long and short months of the year (with the exception of February). More complicated than a simple calendar (which must be adjusted for all months of fewer than thirty-one days), less complicated than a perpetual calendar.

ANTI-MAGNETIC WATCH: A watch with features incorporated into the movement or, more commonly, the case that protects it from disturbances caused by magnetism.

ANTI-REFLECTIVE COATING: A thin metallic coating applied to the crystal to help eliminate glare; usually applied to the inside of the crystal but sometimes to both sides.

APERTURE: An opening on a dial through which can be seen displays such as the date, day, month, or moon phase.

APPLIQUE: Numerals or symbols that are adhered to a dial.

ARBOR: A rotating post (or axle) in a watch movement. Typically the central portion of a wheel (containing the pinion) or the central attachment point of the mainspring; the barrel arbor.

ATM: Refers to a watch's water-pressure rating. ATM is short for atmosphere and roughly the equivalent of ten meters of depth; i.e., a watch with a rating of 1 ATM means it is safe under ten meters of water; a 5 ATM rating means fifty meters.

AUTOMATIC WATCH: A self-winding watch; a watch that does not have to be wound manually. It winds itself by the action of the watch on the wearer's wrist, typically through a semicircular rotor inside the watchcase that winds the mainspring. The rotor winds either in just one direction or two directions. (Some brands prefer one style, some the other; Patek watches usually wind in one direction, Rolexes in both directions.) The automatic movement was first dreamed up by Abraham-Louis Perrelet in 1770, but not successfully put into practice until Englishman John Harwood's 1923 automatic wristwatch prototype.

AUTOMATON: An animated component or character on a watch that performs some action on command, typically associated with a minute repeater or other striking complication, and often depicting erotic scenes. Also known as a Jacquemart.

AVIATOR'S WATCH: Traditionally, a big watch with an oversized dial and luminous numbers and hands; aircraft navigators wore this type of watch with long leather straps over the sleeve, i.e., the watch was worn outside the flight jacket.

BALANCE: The equivalent of a pendulum of a clock in a watch. The balance vibrates back and forth (similar to a pendulum); the vibration produced is determined by the size and weight of the balance combined with the strength and length of the hairspring. The balance, vibrating at a set frequency, controls the watch's timekeeping.

The balance spring (also called the hairspring) makes the balance swing back-and-forth, dividing time into equal parts. Each back-and-forth movement of the balance is called an oscillation. One oscillation is composed of two vibrations.

In modern watches, the rate of the balance wheel (see following entry) is between 18,000 and 36,000 oscillations per hour.

BALANCE WHEEL: The rough equivalent of a pendulum in a clock. Instead of relying on gravity as the restoring force, it uses a spiral-shaped spring (the hairspring).

BALL-BEARING: A bearing that employs stainless steel balls rolling in an enclosed space to reduce friction. Usually found on the rotor of automatic watches, some companies have begun using ceramic ball-bearings; theoretically they are a longer-lasting, more efficient alternative.

BARREL: The watch's power source, and the mechanical equivalent of a battery. The barrel has a large coiled spring that can be wound to transmit the driving force to the power train.

BEAT RATE: The frequency of oscillation of the movement, usually expressed as vibrations (ticks) per hour (VPH) or as a proper frequency in hertz (Hz). Beat error is the symmetry of the "tick" and the "tock" in a mechanical movement; if the vibrations of the balance are perfectly equal in both directions, it is said to be in beat, i.e., it has no beat error.

BEZEL: The ring around a watch's crystal that sometimes holds the crystal in place and sometimes is merely decorative. Bezels are usually static, but can also rotate to make mathematical calculations or keep track of elapsed time.

BI-DIRECTIONAL WINDING: An automatic mechanism that winds the mainspring with the rotor spinning in both the clockwise and counterclockwise directions.

BIG DATE: An oversize date display, typically made up of two overlapping discs for the different digits.

BOMBE: French for "convex." A round, or domed, shape. Sometimes used to describe a specific, bulbous lug shape, i.e., bombe lugs.

BRACELET: A metal watchband, usually in steel or gold.

BREGUET HANDS (also called pomme hands): They feature a straight or slightly leaf-shaped shaft with a small circle and a slightly off-center cutout and a pointed tip.

BREGUET NUMERALS: Numbers designed in the style of Abraham-Louis Breguet.

BREGUET OVERCOIL: See Overcoil hairspring.

BRIDGE: The structure in a watch that usually supports any part of the movement and is secured on two sides; the framework of the watch.

BUBBLE BACK: Early Rolex cases with backs shaped in the form of a slight bubble.

BUMPER WIND: An early version of a modern automatic watch in which the rotor, or the oscillating weight, does not rotate a full 360 degrees but only a portion of that. It sometimes has springs at the end attached to the rotor or frame; when it winds it bumps back and forth between the two springs.

BUTTERFLY CLASP: A watch bracelet or band in which the two ends of the buckle fold over into the center.

CALENDAR WATCH: A watch with a pointer, subdial, or aperture that tells the day of the week, the date, and the month, or some combination of these.

CALIBER: The designation used to indicate different types of movements by a watch manufacturer; usually used in relationship to a number, such as the JLC cal. 889, with the 889 referring to a series of different distinct movements, such as the 889/1 or 889/2. Historically, the caliber number bore some relationship to the diameter of the movement.

CANNON PINION: The friction clutch in a watch movement that allows the hands to be set independently of the motion of the gear train.

CARILLON: A repeater or other striking watch with three or more gongs.

CASE: The metal container holding the watch movement; usually in steel, gold, titanium, or platinum. Older watches were often cased in silver.

CASE BACK: The underside of a watch. Usually signed by the brand, a recent trend has been to make case backs transparent, i.e., featuring a synthetic crystal that allows a view of the movement.

CENTRAL SECONDS (also called sweep seconds): A second hand located in the center of the dial, as opposed to subseconds. Central seconds are divided into two types, direct and indirect, referring to whether the second hand is part of the wheel train's power flow; if not, it is indirect.

CHRONOGRAPH: A watch featuring an additional stopwatch function. Chronographs have two separate, and independent, time systems. One tells the time of day; the other functions like a stopwatch and measures intervals of time. Most modern chronographs have two pushers: One starts and stops the timing; the other resets the hands to zero when the timing is stopped.

CHRONOMETER: To become certified as a chronometer by the Contrôle Officiel Suisse des Chronomètres (COSC), a watch must pass stringent, internationally agreed-upon tests relating to its accuracy. The COSC is a Swiss government agency that tests watches to guarantee they can time within an acceptable error rate. The watch is tested in five different positions (dial up, dial down, crown down, crown left, and crown right) and at temperatures replicating the conditions under which the watch will be worn.

CLOISONNÉ: A decorative enameling technique using tiny threads of gold to separate various colors to create a design or image. Sometimes used for finer watch dials or cases.

COAXIAL: In a loose sense, the term means sharing the same axis. Today the term generally refers to a coaxial escapement, which was invented by George Daniels and recently implemented by Omega.

The coaxial escapement is more complex than the traditional lever escapement; it has more parts and requires more precise adjustment. On the other hand, it is theoretically impervious to the influence of lubrication, the proper condition of which the traditional lever escapement is entirely dependent on. It also features a smaller angle of interaction between the pallet fork and the balance wheel, thus minimizing another disturbing influence to the timekeeping.

COIN WATCH: A watch movement inserted inside a coin, which then serves as the watchcase. Usually the coin, most often an older gold piece, is fitted with lugs and a normal band; sometimes the watch stands alone as a pocket watch. Corum helped pioneer the trend, but other brands have also manufactured them.

COLUMN WHEEL: A control mechanism consisting of a wheel with ratchet teeth on the bottom and vertical columns on top; traditionally it was employed by finer chronograph movements to coordinate the start, stop, and reset functions.

COMPLICATION: A basic watch tells the time; extras such as the day, the date, or the month are generally called complications. Other complications include a chronograph function, a power-reserve indicator, an alarm, and a moon-phase indicator. Rarer, and therefore more valuable, complications include a tourbillon and a repeater.

COSC: Contrôle Officiel Suisse des Chronomètres. See Chronometer.

CÔTES DE GENÈVE: A regular decorative pattern of parallel waves, usually on the movement bridges; sometimes referred to as Geneva stripes.

CROWN: A knob on a watchcase that winds the mainspring in mechanical watches. The crown also sets the time, and at a different position, sometimes the day and date.

CROWN GUARDS (also called horns): Protrusions from the side of the case next to the crown to protect it from getting knocked or bent on sports watches.

CRYSTAL: A transparent cover made of glass, plastic, or synthetic sapphire that protects the dial. (Synthetic sapphire is actually crystallized aluminum oxide.) Although most crystals today are scratch-resistant, they are not scratchproof — they are not as hard as a diamond, and some substances can leave marks.

CURB PINS: The pins on the regulator that restrict the hairspring and control its effective length, consequently determining the rate of the watch. Also known as regulating pins.

CYCLOPS: The small lens on a crystal that magnifies the date making it more readable.

DEMI-HUNTER CASE (also called half-hunter): A protective lid hinged to a watchcase to cover the dial but with a hole in the center large enough so the time can still be read.

DEPLOYANT (also called a folding clasp): A buckle on a watch strap that opens and closes using hinged extenders. Invented by Louis Cartier in 1910, a deployant buckle is easier to fasten than a normal buckle and prevents the watch from falling off the wrist.

DIAL: A watch's face.

DIGITAL DISPLAY: Time shown by using numbers instead of hands on a dial.

DISPLAY BACK: A transparent back that allows the movement to be viewed; usually made of synthetic sapphire.

DOPPELCHRONOGRAPH: See Split-seconds chronograph.

DUAL-TIME WATCH: A watch that displays an additional time zone.

DUO-DIAL WATCHES: Watches with faces divided into two parts; traditionally the hour and minute hands are on top, and the second hand is below.

ÉBAUCHE: Historically this French term meant an unfinished, raw movement with just the main plate, the wheels, and the bridges. More recently it has come to mean anything from a raw movement supplied as a "parts kit" to an entire decorated, assembled, and adjusted movement; often used in reference to manufacturers supplying watch brands with completed movements upon which the latter then put their names.

EQUATION OF TIME: The difference between the clock time and the time defined by the position of the sun. Because we divide the day into twenty-four equal hours, true solar time may differ slightly.

ESCAPEMENT: This most important part of the watch movement serves a dual function — it makes sure the oscillator keeps oscillating, whether in a pendulum-based clock or in a balance-wheel-based mechanical watch, and it also releases the power from the mainspring in very regulated increments that control the motion of the hands and therefore the display of the time.

ESCAPE WHEEL: Driven by the gears in the power train, it regulates the unwinding action of the mainspring and supplies power to the balance wheel via the pallet fork in a lever escapement watch.

FAST-BEAT: Historically, any watch movement with a beat rate higher than 18,000 VPH (vibrations per hour); today it often is applied to movements with 28,800 or 36,000 VPH.

FINISHING: The final step in manufacturing any part or component. A crude or rough surface created by a file or a saw blade is generally said to be unfinished, whereas a highly polished or carefully grained (brushed) and beveled surface is said to be finely finished (depending on how well it's done).

Some finishing details are critical to the proper operation of the part in question and are called functional finishing. Other finishing details are purely decorative and demonstrate the skill of the watchmaker.

Generally when collectors discuss finishing, they're referring to the decorative detailing of the movement or case. There is a complex language of finishing styles and techniques that might be discussed by movement connoisseurs in the same way wine lovers discuss grape varieties, vintages, and *terroir*.

FLYBACK HAND: A term that has two semi-distinct meanings in watchmaking. It can be used to differentiate a flyback chronograph (the chronograph can be instantaneously reset and restarted with a single push of the flyback, or reset, button) from a conventional chronograph, in which you push the start/stop button, the reset button, then the start/stop button again to accomplish the same function.

The term is also often used to describe the reset action of a conventional chronograph or any hand that retrogrades — or returns to a start position with an instantaneous action, i.e., flyback hand, flyback action, flyback function.

FOUDROYANTE: A small dial on a chronograph marked 0 through 8. The small hand on the dial completes a sweep every second, allowing the time to be read in eighths of a second. Foudroyantes have also been produced with 1/4- or 1/5-second readings.

FREE-SPRUNG BALANCE: A balance and hairspring that does not involve a regulator and curb pins; instead, screws, nuts, or inertia blocks on the balance rim alter the moment of inertia of the balance to change the rate.

FULL ROTOR: Automatic watches with oscillating weights, or rotors, that rotate through 360 degrees, to distinguish them from a bumper wind.

GASKET: A formed piece of rubber or nylon (cork and even lead were used in the past as well), designed to prevent water from entering the case.

GEAR TRAIN: An assortment of wheels and pinions that either slow down or speed up the transfer of rotational energy.

GENEVA SEAL: Dating back to 1886, a seal that certifies a watch meets certain standards of quality set by the Canton of Geneva (exclusively for movements produced in Geneva); these standards were revised (and tightened) in 1957.

GLUCYDUR: A trade name for beryllium copper, used to make high-grade balance wheels.

GMT: A watch that displays Greenwich Mean Time in addition to the local time; also called UTC (Coordinated Universal Time).

GOLD-FILLED: Rather than being made of 100-percent gold, a gold-filled case is one in which gold bars are soldered to a base metal, then rolled into sheets, providing a higher thickness of gold than gold-plating.

GRANDE SONNERIE: A watch that strikes hours and quarter hours in passing; typically also accompanied by a minute-repeater function.

GUILLOCHE: The French word for engine turning, used to describe a decoration most commonly found on the surface of a watch dial.

HACKING: A feature that stops the second hand when you pull out the stem to set the time, allowing you to set the time to the second; this is particularly useful when coordinating with a time signal or synchronizing two watches.

HAIRSPRING (also called balance spring): A very thin, spiral-shaped spring; coupled with the balance, it forms the harmonic oscillator that controls the timekeeping in the watch.

HAND: The indicator that moves over the dial to point to the hour, minute, or second. Hands come in a variety of shapes, including baton, Breguet, sword, arrow, and so on.

HUNTER: A watchcase fitted with a front cover that protects the glass.

INCABLOC: A trade name for the most commonly used kind of shock protection.

INTEGRATED BRACELET: A metal watchband incorporated into the watchcase.

ISOCHRONISM: Technically, the extent to which the balance will keep the same rate at varying amplitudes, whether the changes in amplitude are the result of horizontal to vertical positional changes or varying states of wind; generally used to indicate whether a watch keeps the same time when fully wound or half wound, etc.

JEWELS: When referring to movements, jewels are the bearings used to reduce friction. Synthetic rubies are used because of their hardness, which reduces friction and wear. A high number of jewels does not necessarily mean a watch is of higher quality; only a certain number of jewels are needed to allow a watch to perform optimally.

JUMPING HOUR: A watch in which the hour is indicated by a number springing into view, rather than by a hand; also referred to by the French term *heures sautantes*. Less commonly, a traditional hour hand that jumps in one-hour increments precisely at the change of the hour.

KARAT: The measure of gold content. Pure gold is 24 karats; 14 karats means 14 parts of gold and 10 parts of other metals by weight.

KIF: A trade name for a type of shock protection.

LIGHT-EMITTING DIODE (LED): Used in digital displays on electronic quartz watches.

LIQUID-CRYSTAL DISPLAY (LCD): The electronic display of time, achieved by using a thin layer of liquid held between two plates.

LNIB: Abbreviation for "like new in box"; used when selling watches.

LUGS: The projections on the watchcase that hold the spring bars used to attach a strap or bracelet.

LUMINOVA: A trade name for a non-radioactive luminous material used for watch dials and hands; now replaced by Super-LumiNova.

MAIN PLATE: Essentially, the chassis of the watch; the base plate on which all the other parts of a watch movement are mounted.

MAINSPRING: A watch's power supply, coiled up inside the barrel. When unwound, a common mainspring is about nine to thirteen inches. The longer the mainspring, the longer the power reserve.

MANUAL WIND: Wound by hand, using the crown.

MANUFACTURE: The French word meaning a company that produces at least one movement in-house.

MECHANICAL WATCH: A watch that runs from the energy released by its spring rather than electricity.

MICROROTOR: An automatic watch with a small, decentralized rotor, typically recessed within the movement for extra thinness.

MILITARY TIME: Time measured in twenty-four-hour segments; for example, 8:15 PM would be 20:15.

MINERAL CRYSTAL: A watch crystal made of mineral glass, which is cheaper and less durable than synthetic sapphire.

MINUTE REPEATER: A watch that strikes the time on command using different dings and dongs for hours and minutes: There is one tone for each hour, a double tone for each quarter hour, and another higher or lower tone for each minute; for example, Ding Ding Ding, Ding Dong, Dong Dong Dong Dong indicates that the time is 3:19). Invented by Englishman Daniel Quare in 1690, it was an important device before watches could be read in the dark. Now it's a demonstration of watchmaking artistry.

MODULE: A complication that can be attached to a base movement as a complete unit. Chronographs, perpetual calendars, astronomical displays, and repeaters can all be modular in design.

MONOPUSHER: A chronograph with only one pusher for the start, stop, and reset functions.

MOON-PHASE INDICATOR: A watch complication that displays the phases of the moon either through an aperture or, less commonly, with a small hand.

MOVEMENT: Basically, a watch's engine. It consists of the winding mechanism, the mainspring, the train, the escapement, and the regulating elements.

NIB: Stands for "new in box," and it means the watch is new (as opposed to LNIB).

NIVAROX: A trade name for a hairspring alloy with superior temperature-compensating properties, available in varying grades: I, II, etc.

NOS: Stands for "new old stock," a watch that has never been used, or even sold, although it can be many decades old.

OSCILLATING SYSTEM: The oscillating system is formed by the hairspring and the balance. Two vibrations of the balance create the ticking sound of a mechanical watch, known as one oscillation.

OVERCOIL HAIRSPRING: A hairspring where the final (or terminal) curve is elevated above the plane of the rest of the spring.

PALLETS: The central component of the escapement, also known as the lever, pallet lever, or pallet fork, alternately locks and receives impulse from the escape wheel and is unlocked by and provides impulse to the balance via the roller jewel.

PATINA: Discoloration of a dial or hands, which is usually due to age.

PERLAGE: A decorative surface treatment of small overlapping circles applied primarily to bridges or the visible portions of the main plate. Also referred to as spotting.

PERPETUAL CALENDAR: A complication that adjusts itself automatically for different month lengths and leap years.

Perpetual calendars are programmed to be accurate until the year 2100.

PILOT'S WATCH: See Aviator's watch.

PINION: The smaller, geared portion of a wheel; pinions have "leaves" where wheels have "teeth."

PLATE: Often the main plate, the primary piece supporting the movement's various parts and bridges. The bottom side of a plate is the dial side, the top side the bridge side. Sometimes the word plate is used interchangeably with bridge or sometimes refers to smaller, thin coverings or fixtures in a movement.

POWER RESERVE: The length of time a watch will run from fully wound until it stops.

POWER-RESERVE INDICATOR: A subdial that shows how much power remains before a watch stops running.

PULSOMETER: A scale on the dial or bezel of a watch that, with the second hand, can be used to measure a person's pulse rate.

PUSHER: A button on a watchcase that activates a function like the chronograph start/stop or reset, an alarm on/off switch, or a quick-set date corrector.

QUARTER REPEATER: A striking watch that chimes the time on command to the quarter hour. See also Minute repeater.

QUARTZ CRYSTAL: The piece of quartz that serves as an oscillator in a quartz watch.

QUARTZ WATCH: An electric watch regulated by a quartz oscillator.

QUICK-SET DATE: A mechanism that allows the user to set the date directly via the crown or a pusher to avoid having to turn the hands over many times.

RADIUM: A radioactive material formerly applied to watch hands and dials to make them glow in the dark. Due to health concerns, it is no longer used.

RATCHET WHEEL: The wheel attached to the barrel arbor that winds and maintains the mainspring power in conjunction with the click.

RATTRAPANTE: See Split-seconds chronograph.

REGULATION: The act of altering the daily rate of the watch by means of moving the regulator (curb pins) or the adjustable masses on the balance (in the case of a free-sprung balance).

REGULATOR: Most commonly, the part of the movement that alters the rate of the watch by changing the position of the curb pins and the effective length of the hairspring.

Also, a watch or clock with the hours and minutes (and seconds) indications separated (non-coaxial). Also known as the index.

REMONTOIRE: A device that ensures a consistent amount of power is supplied to the escapement to improve the isochronism; it generally consists of a secondary power source somewhere in the power train or even on the escapement itself that is periodically rewound by the mainspring. (Remontoir is French for "rewind.")

RESONATING BALANCE WHEELS: A set of two balances or pendulums housed within the same structure, designed to vibrate in harmony with each other. Theoretically, some of the imperfections inherent in a watch's hairspring and escapement will be experienced in opposition (if one balance gains time in a certain position, the other one will lose time in the same position). The balances should maintain a sympathetic vibration with each other; that is, should they deviate when disturbed, whether from shocks or positional variations, the imbalances will average out.

RETROGRADE HANDS: Hands that jump backward and begin again when they reach their last indication; for example, a watch with retrograde seconds will reach sixty on a scale, jump back to zero, and start again.

REPEATER: See Minute repeater.

REVERSO: A watchcase that can be turned over within the frame. Although many brands, including Hamilton and Chronoswiss, have sold models, JLC developed the Reverso and still manufactures far more models than any other company.

RHODIUM: A hard, bright silver-white metal often used to electroplate white gold cases because of its chromelike appearance.

ROLLED GOLD: A thin sheet of gold bonded to a base metal. See also Gold-filled.

ROTOR: A chunk of metal that swivels on an axis and transmits winding energy to an automatic watch's mainspring.

Each time it moves it advances the ratchet wheel, which keeps the spring wound.

ROSE GOLD: Gold with a slightly reddish color caused by additional copper in the alloy. Rose gold, red gold, and pink gold are all slightly different alloys with varying amounts of copper and other constituent elements.

SCREW BACK: A back that is able to be screwed into the case, as opposed to watch backs that are screwed in through the use of small screws or are snapped on.

SCREW-DOWN CROWN: A crown that screws down into the case to make a watch more water- and dust-resistant.

SECOND TIME-ZONE INDICATOR: An additional dial that can be set to another time zone.

SHOCK ABSORBER: Typically used on the balance pivots, allowing them to shift slightly in their position during shocks without breaking the pivots.

SHOCK-RESISTANT: The ability to withstand an impact equal to a three-foot fall onto a wooden floor.

SKELETON WATCH: A watch whose movement has had much of the material for the plates, bridges, and sometimes even wheels and barrel removed to expose more of the mechanism.

SMALL SECONDS: Seconds displayed by a hand in a small subsidiary dial.

SONNERIE: A watch that sounds the time automatically; a petite sonnerie chimes every hour, a grande sonnerie every quarter hour.

SPLIT-SECONDS CHRONOGRAPH: A chronograph that employs two chronograph second hands to measure elapsed time as well as lap time. In other words, one chronograph hand can be stopped while the other keeps ticking; you can then record time and hit the catch-up button, and the stopped hand will catch up to the next. Also known as rattrapante or doppelchronograph.

SPRING BAR: A thin metal bar with spring-loaded extensions mounted between the lugs that attach a strap or bracelet to the case.

STEM: The shaft that connects to the movement's winding mechanism. The crown is fitted to the opposite end.

STRIKING WATCH: A watch with an acoustic complication such as a minute repeater or sonnerie that is struck on a gong.

SUBDIAL: A small dial placed inside a watch's main dial. These dials often hold complications such as chronograph counters, an alarm indication, or a second time-zone indicator.

SWAN'S-NECK REGULATOR: A traditional form of micro-regulator that allows very precise adjustment of the rate. It employs a screw for adjusting the position of the regulator and a long, curved spring (shaped something like a swan's neck) to hold the regulator firmly against the tip of the screw.

SWEEP-SECONDS HAND: A second hand mounted in the center of a dial.

SWISS MADE: A watch can be considered Swiss if its movement is at least 50-percent Swiss (by value), its movement is assembled in Switzerland, and the manufacturer carries out a final technical inspection in Switzerland.

TACHYMETER: A device used on a chronograph for calculating speed over a measured distance or the hourly productivity of any event that takes less than one minute. When a car on the highway passes a mile marker, a passenger starts the chronograph. When the car passes the next mile marker the chronograph is stopped. If the chronograph's seconds hand points to 75 on the tachymeter scale, this indicates the car's speed is 75 miles per hour.

TANG BUCKLE: The traditional strap attachment involving a pin (called a tang) and buckle.

TANTALUM: A rare blue-gray metal used to make a variety of strong alloys with very high melting points, sometimes used in its pure form for watchcases. Because it is not affected by sweat and other body secretions, it is non-irritating.

TELEMETER: A chronograph scale for measuring distance based on the time it takes the sound to reach the observer.

THREE-PIECE CASE: A traditional watchcase consisting of a case middle, bezel, and back.

TIME-ONLY WATCH: A watch that tells the time without any complications, such as a chronograph or a date watch.

TITANIUM: A family of gray, hypoallergenic metal alloys containing the element titanium; it is stronger and lighter than stainless steel and is an increasingly popular choice for cases and bracelets.

TONNEAU: A watchcase shaped like a barrel.

TOURBILLON: Invented by Abraham-Louis Breguet in 1801, it is a rotating cage within the watch that contains the balance, hairspring, and escapement. Traditionally it rotates once every minute (although versions with different time frames are not uncommon) and is designed to eliminate positional errors in the vertical positions. As it rotates, it exposes each positional error for the same amount of time, thus averaging them out.

TRAIN: A series of wheels in a watch or clock; the power train or gear train.

TRICOMPAX: A chronograph with three subdials at three, six, and nine o'clock.

TRIPLE CALENDAR: A dial displaying the day, date, and month.

TRITIUM: A slightly radioactive substance used to make hands or hour markers glow in the dark. Super-LumiNova, a non-radioactive substance, is slowly replacing tritium.

TWO-TONE: A watchcase made of two metals of different colors, typically steel and gold.

UNI-DIRECTIONAL WINDING: An automatic mechanism that only winds the mainspring when the rotor is turning in one direction.

UP-AND-DOWN INDICATOR: Indicates power reserve.

WATCH WINDER: An electric device that stores and winds automatic watches when the watch isn't in use. Typically, a watch winder should give just enough energy to make a watch run for twenty-four hours in any given day. It is particularly useful for a perpetual calendar, or some other complex astronomical complication, where it is overly labor intensive to constantly reset the watch.

WATER-RESISTANT: The ability to withstand water pressure. Water resistance is measured in meters and refers to the depth that the watch will keep out water.

WHEEL: The circular gear revolving around an axis, which transmits power or motion.

WHITE GOLD: Any alloy of gold that is white in color, usually with nickel or palladium.

MISCELLANY

Books

Braun, Peter. *Wristwatch Annual 2005: The Catalog of Producers, Models, and Specifications*. New York: Abbeville, 2005.

Brunner, Gisbert L., and Christian Pfeiffer-Belli. *Swiss Watches: Chronology of Worldwide Success*. West Chester, PA: Schiffer Publishing Ltd, 1991.

Brunner, Gisbert L., and Christian Pfeiffer-Belli. *Wristwatches*. Koln: Konemann, 1999.

Brunner, Gisbert L., and Christian Pfeiffer-Belli. *Wristwatches: A Handbook and Price Guide*. Atglen, PA: Schiffer Publishing, 1993.

Childers, Caroline, and Roberta Naas. *Master Wristwatches*. New York: BW Publishing, 1999.

Christianson, David. *Timepieces: Masterpieces of Chronology*. Buffalo, NY: Firefly Books, 2002.

Cutmore, Max. *Collecting and Repairing Watches*. London: David & Charles, 1999.

Edwards, Frank. *Wristwatches: A Connoisseur's Guide*. Buffalo, NY: Firefly Books, 1997.

Kahlert, Helmut, Richard Mühle, and Gisbert L. Brunner. *Wristwatches: History of a Century's Development*. Munich: Schiffer Publishing Ltd, 1983.

Korda, Michael. *Marking Time: Collecting Watches—and Thinking about Time*. New York: Barnes & Noble Books, 2004.

Lander, David S. *Revolution in Time*. rev. ed. Cambridge, MA: Belknap Press, 2000.

Lange, Walter. *The Revival of Time: Memoirs*. Berlin: Econ, 2005.

Negretti, Giampiero, and Paolo De Vecchi. *Patek Philippe: Complicated Wristwatches,* Milan: Könemann, 1997.

Pannier, Rene. *Collectible Watches*. Paris: Flammarion, 2001.

Rondeau, Rene. *Hamilton Wristwatches: A Collector's Guide*. Corte Madera, CA: Rene Rondeau, 1999.

Shugart, Cooksey, Tom Engle, and Richard E. Gilbert. *Complete Price Guide to Watches*. 25th ed. Paducah, KY: Collector Books, 2005.

Sobel, Dava. *Longitude: The Story of a Lone Genius Who Solved the Greatest Scientific Problem of His Time*. New York: Walker, 1995.

Traub, Lucien F. *The World of Watches: History, Technology, Industry*. New York: Ebner Publishing International, 2005.

Magazines and Websites

Not long ago there were no magazines dedicated to the wristwatch; now there are several. Among these are *Watch-Time*, *International Watch*, *Hr: Watches*, *InSync*, and *Chronos*.

A vast number of Websites dedicated to watches have also recently appeared. Some of these are excellent sources of knowledge that might otherwise be nearly impossible to find on your own; some are traps filled with misinformation. Among the best sites are EquationofTime.com, ThePuristS.com, TimeZone.com, and WatchUSeek.com.

Many retailers have Websites; but be careful. As mentioned, it is generally best to buy a watch after you've seen it. Still, many of the more respected stores do post excellent photographs of both the exteriors and the interiors of watches, and offer solid returns programs as well. And there are certain outfits that do almost all their business on eBay or other auction sites. Here you must be careful to bid only when you are confident that the seller is trustworthy. Even experienced buyers have been taken online. But at the same time, it's also possible to find exactly the watch you want at a great price. And many retail stores offer a great deal of information about watches and brands on their sites, much of which can be very helpful when making purchases.

INDEX

CREDITS

ACKNOWLEDGMENTS

There are two writers whose books everyone interested in watches should read: David S. Landes, author of *Revolution in Time*, and Lucien F. Trueb, who wrote *The World of Watches: History, Technology, Industry*. The former is the best history of the relationship between humans and timepieces, the latter is a marvelous encyclopedic stash of information about the watch business. Both were essential in writing this book, as were countless people who helped me from the initial planning stages through completion. I am particularly grateful to a few of these who, for various reasons, did not want their name mentioned, but who contributed far more than they could possibly imagine.

I would also like to thank: Jay Adlersberg, Robert Anbian, Michael Ashton, Paul Boutros, Martin Braun, Greg Burghart, George Cramer, Ron deCorte, Mark Doogue, Alan Emtage, Josh Feiner, Michael Friedberg, Steve Gurevitz, Ed Hahn, John Homans, Jason Keanle, Jeffrey Kingston, Mark Kolitz, Alkis Kotsopolous, Jonathan Lesser, Erich Lorenz, Mort Janklow, Felipe Jordão, Erich Lorenz, Thomas Mao, Matthew Morse, John-Paul Newport, Pierre Nobs, Walt Odets, Michael Rhodes, Luc Rosseel, Michael Sandler, Lorena Sicilia, Keith Strandberg, Michael S. Tanney, Oscar Waldan, and Vincent Yeh.

Steve Gurevitz and Michael Sandler deserve a second thank-you for their photographic expertise. I am also indebted to Edward Faber, of Manhattan's Aaron Faber Gallery, for the generous gift of his time, his watches, and his premises. Most of all, this book would not exist without the assistance of Osvaldo Patrizzi and Bernard Bieger at Antiquorum; both the publisher and I are grateful for their kind help with so many of the photographs in this book.

Also very valuable collecting photographs were: Deniz Cakmur, Patrick Colpron, John Gauch, Patrick Geering, Alistair Gibbons, Marcus Hanke, Ty Maitland, Bryan Mintz, René Rondeau, Will Roseman, Ching Yee Sing, Dan Sievenpiper, Kenneth Worley, Laurence Yap, Thomas Yeo, and Nancy Grubb.

Numerous people at many watch companies were also extremely helpful, especially: Dina Behar, Marina Cellitti, Isabelle Corigny, Allison Gottlieb, Hilary Heard, Susanne Herz, Beth Hopping, Rachèle Mongazon, Pierre Nobs, Thomas Prescher, and Mattias Willener. Above all, I would like to express my gratitude to that most accommodating and effective watch professional, Joseph Panetta.

At Abrams, I would like to thank Miko McGinty, Rita Jules, Tricia Levi, Anet Sirna-Bruder, and Aiah Wieder, as well as my very gifted and extraordinarily patient editor, Eric Himmel, without whom this book would not and could not have happened.

Finally, my eternal gratitude to Edwards Johann IV.

Gene Stone